THE MONEY MANAGERS

The Money Managers

EDITED BY

Gilbert Edmund Kaplan
and Chris Welles

WITH AN INTRODUCTION BY

'Adam Smith'

RANDOM HOUSE · NEW YORK

Acknowledgments

THIS BOOK IS ESSENTIALLY a cooperative effort, representing the talents and energies of a considerable number of people.

All of the profiles are based on articles which originally appeared in *The Institutional Investor*. So the first acknowledgment is appropriately to my associate George J. W. Goodman, who played a key role in assisting in the original selection of the money managers to be profiled. Over a third of the book is written by Chris Welles, my coeditor, and the remainder was written by Warren Berry, Stanley Brown, Heidi Fiske, Peter Landau, Wyndam Robertson, Arlo Sederberg and Lee Silberman. Assistance in updating the articles and producing additional research material was provided by Nancy Belliveau, Julie Hedges, Solveig Jansson and Penelope Orth. Valuable assistance in preparing the manuscript came from Sibyl Fulenwider and Elizabeth Langdon.

Finally, thanks is due to the nineteen men portrayed here, who graciously submitted to intensive interviewing and critical analysis. Without their cooperation, this book obviously would have been impossible.

GILBERT EDMUND KAPLAN
Editor-in-Chief
The Institutional Investor

The game of professional investment is intolerably boring and overexacting to anyone who is entirely exempt from the gambling instinct; whilst he who has it must pay to this propensity the appropriate toll.

—John Maynard Keynes

Contents

INTRODUCTION
by 'Adam Smith'

BY NOW it must be reasonably well known that the money business is not exactly the way it used to be. If it were still the same we wouldn't have this book.

First of all, in the olden days—say a generation ago—we didn't have this profession of the money manager, or at least we didn't think of it that way. Of course, there have always been professional money managers. If you go to the Baker Library at the Harvard Business School and ask nicely, they may show you the account books of the Medicis, with instructions to and reports from various agents and managers, all done in a flowing medieval Italian script. (The librarians told me it was medieval Italian script. I can't read medieval Italian script. The books are *very old*, and have strange symbols in the margins. The young tigers upstairs boning up for MERC—Managerial Economics, Reporting and Control—probably don't even realize that what they are boning up on has marvelous Renaissance antecedents in the basement.)

Only a generation ago, a money manager was a Prudent Man. If you ran your own money, you could behave any way you liked within the limits of the laws, and sometimes those limits were fuzzy. But if you managed someone else's money as a fiduciary, then you had to be a Prudent Man. The phrase comes from a famous case in 1831, *Amory vs. Harvard College,* and the test was that the fiduciary act "as would any Prudent Man." What did a Prudent Man do? He conserved, in the original meaning of the word. His mission was to preserve and continue and protect the capital entrusted to him. Over the years, a whole manner and costume evolved. It wasn't required, but within memory Prudent Men wore vests, ate breakfast and lunched at the Club, and died with estates that won the approval and admiration of their executors—also Prudent Men. Generally, the Prudent Men bought bonds and the stocks of the two hundred biggest companies in the United States—because any court would have agreed that that is how any Prudent Man would act.

There are still Prudent Men around, but they are having a harder time. For one thing, nearly all the bonds outstanding in this country at this writing have lost money for their purchasers. That's what inflation will do for you. If you hold bonds with a 4 per cent coupon and interest rates go up and money gets tight, new bonds come out at 6 per cent and yours go down until they, too, yield 6 per cent. So, in the past generation, the bond-buying Prudent Man turned out not to be so Prudent. He failed in his charter: to preserve the capital. (Bonds *can* go down, too. One can, of course, wait until the bonds mature and get paid off at 100 cents on the dollar, but the dollars invested will have lost large fractions of their purchasing power by that time.) Buying the two hundred biggest companies and locking them away hasn't worked that well either, although that procedure too is legally immune from court criticism. Just recently someone went to court to protest about a fiduciary who bought only bonds. The protester claimed that, even though that might have been prudent in the days of *Amory vs. Harvard College,* it wasn't prudent any more because it wasn't preserving the capital—you had to take inflation into account. All of this is just to say that the concept of prudence has changed, and so have investment philosophies.

Now we live in the Age of Performance. Performance means, quite simply, that your portfolio does better than the others. If the market goes up, the performance portfolio goes up more. If the market goes down, the performance portfolio goes down less. You average this out over both up and down markets, and if your portfolio doesn't meet those standards, they take away your performance card.

The chief factor in bringing about the Age of Performance has been the failure of the traditional prudent management to preserve the purchasing power of the portfolio. But there are at least two other important factors.

One is the age of the managers. You will notice that most of the managers discussed in this book are young—in their thirties and forties. The senior generation, which witnessed 1929 firsthand, has retired or is approaching retirement. From 1929 to 1947 only a few hardy souls ventured into the money business. A friend of mine who went to the Street in 1937 said that on summer days on Wall Street things were so quiet that, walking down that famous canyon, all you could hear through the open windows was the rattle of backgammon dice. In short, there is a generation missing, and the new generation has moved into positions of responsibility much more quickly than it would have on the old timetable. The new generation has achieved its status by ignoring the favorite precepts of the old.

A second factor has been the institutionalization of investments. You will notice that money managers in this book are not famous traders for their own accounts like, say, Jesse Livermore, Ben Smith or even Joseph Kennedy. For the most part they are managers of mutual funds. A mutual fund that has a superior track record provides its salesmen with good ammunition. They sell more shares of the fund, the management fees increase, and all those associated with the fund make more money. So the pressure is on to perform. Mutual fund assets themselves have grown from $1.3 billion in 1946 to $56.9 billion in 1968. The performance of the mutual funds influences the managers of state and corporate pension funds, which now total $55 billion, and of insurance companies, which now have $10 billion in common stocks. In short, the market is more and more a professional market.

Most of these professionals no longer think of their mission as preserving capital; they think of it as *making money.* Those are two sharply different states of mind. Of course, these are managers of aggressive funds, for the most part—not trust officers who must be available to the needs of widows and orphans. But they have an influence even on the trust officers, and that influence is the philosophy that preserving the capital is no way to manage money. Money should *make* money.

Given this, there is one other great difference between the managers of the Age of Performance and what had gone before. The Prudent Men acted as a group. Investment decisions were made by the Investment Committee. The institutions spoke with the royal We: "We believe that patience will reward the prudent investor . . ."

The managers of the Age of Performance are individuals. They operate as individuals and their portfolios reflect their personal feelings and philosophies. If they are investment counselors, they insist that their clients give them discretion and a totally free hand. If they are portfolio managers in a bank or an insurance company, their bosses—and they do have bosses—leave them alone. It is a tenet of the new Age of Performance that only individuals can make decisions. The individual may get his information from a hundred sources, may consult with a dozen colleagues, may be responsible to a whole host of people, but the responsibility—and the record—are his own. A committee is merely a way of delaying decisions and fuzzing up the responsibility, according to the tenets of Performance.

With individual responsibility so visible in a field where results are so easily tracked, the team facade of the dignified committee began to be eclipsed, and the Stars were born. It seems to be the age of the Joe Namaths, and in fact, the star portfolio manager is much like a pro quarterback: he is under continuous pressure, he must perform all the time, he is paid inordinately better than the plodding, plugging team members and if he gets intercepted too often he doesn't stay a star. And a star can earn a million dollars a year.

Are these stars really smarter than all the rest of us? "It's not that we're any smarter," says Fred Alger, whom you will find here as one of the stars, "it's that we work at it, minute by minute, all day long." Now, I know most of the gentlemen contained herein, and I can vouch for this. They do work at it all day long, but it doesn't seem like work, because the quest for the new and fresh idea—the stock that will outperform the others—is an exciting game. "Oh, beautiful, baby, beautiful," says David Meid, as someone reads some nubile, bewitching numbers to him over the phone. So it is not just that the professional managers get more information than the amateur investor, though this is indeed true. The professional manager can remember the earnings histories of several hundred companies, the way their stocks respond to certain kinds of news, and he needs only one seemingly insignificant piece of incremental information to push this apperceptive mass, as the psychologists call it, over the line to a decision. In short, he is really at his job seven days a week because he thinks about the market all the time. It turns him on.

Not only that, but the good professional abstracts the *process* of decision-making and keeps analyzing it. As John Hartwell puts it, in a rather Harvard Business School-y way, "Organizing for performance means identifying the characteristics that have produced good performance, avoiding extraneous elements, and maximizing the use of all necessary steps." Some of the managers keep special track of their mistakes, to see why they made them and how they can avoid repeating them. In fact, this recognition of mistakes is one of the distinguishing marks of the pro. Amateurs have their egos more involved, and are slower to correct their boners. At least that's the way the mythology goes. Not that the pros aren't without their own little prejudices. Carl Hathaway, who helps to run some $9 billion at the Morgan bank, doesn't like companies run by fat men. (Recently I asked about a company in his portfolio run by a gentleman of some girth and weight. Had he made an exception? Was this just a gag? "No," Carl said, "he's just chubby.")

If these managers work seven days a week and they are so turned on and so damn smart, what can they do for us? In other words, what *is* good performance in the Age of Performance? I asked a dispassionate observer—my wife. I said I was doing a preface to a book about new, smart money managers. "Say you had the smartest one," I said, "what would you expect your account to do?" "The smartest one should double my money, easy," said my wife. It sounds easy, but if you have a $10,000 account, and a money manager can double it every year, you have a fellow with a turban and a wispy tail who comes out of a lamp when you rub it. Because doubling that $10,000 every year for ten years would give you $10,240,000—and that's a pretty optimistic assumption. My wife thought $10 million for $10,000 was nice but perhaps not reasonable, so I tried another exercise: now the account is $50,000, the growth rate is only 60 per cent—reinvested and compounded—and we let it run for twenty years. Figure it out. You have $1,500,000,000 or so—a billion and a half—and are on your way literally to owning the country.

None of these gentlemen, I believe, would claim they could make money grow consistently at 50 per cent compounded per year. They aren't magicians, and they do make mistakes. So that gives you the high end for the scale of expectations.

Anyway, here they are. You can probably learn something from these money managers. If I had to tip you off as to what to look for, I would say look at their attitude toward their mistakes. Look how they get their information, for they don't do that much original work themselves. Look how they believe that good selling is more difficult than good buying. And finally, look how competitive they are. The money they make or lose is almost irrelevant; it is simply the way of keeping score. What is important is to win, to be the best.

There are problems that come from this Age of Performance, just as there were from the Age of Prudence, and it isn't the function of this introduction to go into them. Suffice it to say that this is the way it is, and it will keep on being this way until another age and another generation, to whom all the reasons for change will be obvious.

'Adam Smith'

THE STARS

1

Introduction

WHAT MAKES A STAR? Talent? Looks? Some indefinable aura? In some ways the stock market is much like the movie business in that it is often difficult to explain precisely why one man possesses the knack of picking good stocks, while another does not. Whatever it is, the men in this section have that knack. But what elevates them from being merely extremely proficient money managers to stardom and the placement of their names in lights atop the marquee is their success in the hottest competition on Wall Street: the highly publicized, widely discussed "performance derby" between mutual funds.

Winners of the derby—those mutual funds that score the best gain at the end of each year—receive not only accolades but a fast flow of money from eager investors. As befits stars, many fund managers are paid incredible amounts of money, often more than a million dollars a year. If you want Paul Newman for your movie you have to pay for him, because he is the only Paul Newman there is.

While all of these men have done very well, their personalities, motivations, styles, modes of operation all vary widely. Nothing is more pleasurable to *Dave Meid* than a fresh whiff of hot information, and his response is intuitive and immediate, rather than deliberate and scientific. *Fred Mates* doesn't care how good the story is if the company profits from the war in Vietnam. *Fred Alger* doesn't care so much how well his fund performs as long as it beats the competition. *Fred Carr* doesn't care so much about the competition as he does about building a big empire, and he buys a much different type of stock from anyone else. *Coe Scruggs* regards the market as, more than anything else, a great esthetic experience.

These men are united, though, in their understanding that stardom is ephemeral, that their knack for today's market may not work tomorrow. Many of them have already experienced temporary setbacks. They are all ruthlessly critical of themselves as they try to expunge their weaknesses and keep their lights on the marquee burning brightly.

DAVE MEID
Nirvana from
a beautiful story

LIKE A ROCK FREAK GROOVING on a recording of Big Brother and the Holding Company, David Meid is in an extended, ethereal state of beatitude. He is sagging backward in his chair, his feet draped over the edge of his desk, his shoulders and neck clenching a telephone, his hands playing with the handles of a pair of scissors, and on his face is a smile of true incandescence. "Hey, buddy, it really feels that good, huh?" "No foolin! Is that what he said?" He emits a soft, shrill whistle between his teeth, "$4.25 next year?" He snaps the scissors together a couple of times, rapidly. "And they're the first with the idea, huh?" Another whistle, louder.

Meid is listening—no, not just listening but absorbing, enveloping, like an amoeba envelops its food, substance being directly added to the organism—to that great passport to

utter nirvana, the truly good story, the perfect blending together of happy circumstances which, in a brief time, will
surely cause the stock of a particular company to rise swiftly
in price in relation to its neighbors.

In about five minutes, Meid will have heard about as much
of the story as he wants. That sizzling, vital core of hot data
already will have been revealed, and the "source" on the
other end of the wire will, if he persists, be quickly discouraged from extraneous embellishments. Meid may well call
another source to check the story a little further, but often
he will place an order on the spot, while the story is new and
fresh, and that first, sweet surge of nirvana lasts.

Such a substantial number of the stories that have turned
Meid on have had real substance to them that Meid, who runs
the San Francisco-based Winfield Growth Fund, has become,
at the go-go age of thirty-four, one of the top performers in
the business. In 1967, Winfield gained 100 per cent, not far
behind Fred Carr's Enterprise Fund, though last year it did
slump down the list, gaining a mere 16.4 per cent. Still, his
performance has consistently far outstripped the Dow Jones
Industrial Average and as of the end of 1968 Winfield's assets
were $230 million, a six-fold increase in the past twelve
months.

Meid's involvement with the process of sniffing out stories
is total. He thinks, cares, talks, dreams about little else. besides the market. He is up before seven A.M. in his modest
two-story colonial house in Hillsborough, down the peninsula
from San Francisco, where he lives with his brunette wife,
Lynn, and their three young children. He is soon on the phone
with his Eastern sources. He spends the morning at home
("where I can be free of interruptions"), finally making it

into his tiny corner office on Montgomery Street around noon, after the local closing of the market. (He is fondly looking forward, however, to Winfield's new offices high in the Bank of America building, now under construction, where he will have a contemplative, Jack Dreyfus-like view of the open water.) He is likely to keep going on the phone until he retires, close to midnight.

"I love to pick stocks more than anything else I can imagine," he says. "I'm sometimes amazed that I can actually get paid for doing something that I enjoy so much."

"Dave is the most intense man I have ever met, and also probably the biggest bore. That's why he's so good," says H. L. Jamieson, fifty-five, president of the fund, with not a little of that special kind of reverent awe the old often show for the precocity of the young. "Take the average trust officer of a bank. He thinks about stocks from two until five, then goes home, probably bitching about his long day. But Dave is going all the time, every waking minute."

"Sometimes when I'm talking with him, I stop getting any verbal responses, and I know he's gone," says Bob Hagopian, director of sales for the fund. "I can walk away for ten minutes and he won't even know I've left. Once we were down in LA watching the Dodgers getting whipped in the Series. It was fantastic—Willie Davis was dropping fly balls all over the place and the crowd was screaming—and Dave turned to me and said, 'What do you think we ought to do about those airlines?'"

The reason for Meid's involvement is that, to him, his investment success is the principal means for "taking the measure of myself." He sees running a fund as a precise determination, every market day, of just how good he is.

"There's none of this indefiniteness of whether you did a good job or not," he declares. "You're up or you're down, and there's no room for excuses."

Like most successful young fund managers, he is extremely conscious of his standing vis-à-vis the other funds. And also, like the others, he is brutally frank with himself and with others about his own mistakes and failings. He will analyze at length why Fred Carr of the Enterprise Fund (see p. 33) beat him in 1967, for example, but there will never be mention of luck. He will describe how Carr acted on stories that he did not; how Carr was better able to do this or that. "If a guy beats you," says Meid, "you have to find out why. What does he have that you don't?"

After a couple of recent months, when Winfield was, in Meid's term, "out of phase with the market," he analyzed his complete money-management record to root out weaknesses and the reasons he had missed stories. He closely questioned his staff on where they thought he had gone wrong. "When the fund goes down," says Hagopian, "Dave takes it as a personal insult. I don't have to look at *The Wall Street Journal* to see how the fund is doing. I just look at his face." "It really hits you when one of your favorite stocks gets bagged," Meid says. "It can make you a little defensive for a while and you have to learn to shake it off."

He is just as harsh with the people around him. "Dave is tough on the analysts who don't produce for him," declares an associate. "He demands complete perfection or else." Says Meid, "You have to handle your sources like a baseball manager. You give them money when they're hot, and you treat them with kid gloves."

He treats his portfolio the same way. Several times a day he will jot down that moment's ideal portfolio, his twenty favorite stocks, and next to it, labeled "Sell," the ones in which he is losing confidence. He spends at least twenty minutes daily perusing a computer read-out of the percentage and dollar changes in every one of his positions. "The beauty of stocks is the ability to correct mistakes quickly," he maintains. "You substitute a good-looking stock for one that doesn't work." But this results in a very high turnover ratio— around 2¼ last year—and he is constantly nagged by the feeling that he has sold prematurely. Of his ten largest holdings on June 30, 1967 (including Liquidonics, Monogram Industries, Alloys Unlimited, Teledyne, Solitron Devices), only a single one—Occidental Petroleum—remained in the portfolio a year later, and even that was quickly discarded.

Meid readily admits, "I am basically buy-oriented," and that sales are often made to make way for something that looks better. In a sense, this orientation, he feels, is one of his principal strengths. "The good managers," he says, "are always great bulls because they are the ones to see the potential. Good stocks always sound too good to be true, but lots of times they are that good or better. Really, I'm a fantastic optimist. I'm all offense. I don't neglect the downside, but I'm much more concerned about how I bounce back with the market turns." He points out that during bad times almost everyone is bunched together between 5 and 20 per cent down, but that during good times the top managers really step way out above the so-so ones.

One of Meid's biggest winners has been a company called King Resources, a hustling Denver firm that, among other things, has developed a system of computerized geological analysis of all holes being drilled for oil, and has sold the service to many of the top oil companies. It had been the belief in Denver, however, that John King, head of the company, was a risky man to have one's money on. "A lot of people said he was one of the greatest oil promoters, which is very true," says Meid. "They also expressed doubt he could be trusted, which simply is not true. I found that the skepticism in Denver was due mainly to local jealousy." Feeling King was solid, Meid bought in around 8. The stock recently sold close to 80, and was Winfield's biggest position.

Meid's propensity to believe is unsullied by more traditional forms of security analysis. He rarely, if ever, reads printed research reports ("Most are written by cub analysts who figure it's publish or perish, and most of them are generally late—by the time the report is written, the information has already been discounted"), hardly ever visits company managements, employs no in-house research staff. He relies almost entirely on "soul session" conversations with his sources, and on his daily scanning of the closing prices to spot trends and movement.

Meid, in fact, has only a vaguely formed philosophy of investment. "I'm paid to make decisions, not to justify them," he insists. His single aim is to "be in phase with the best performing stocks," whether they are oceanography stocks or utilities. "If the blue chips are moving, we'll buy blue chips," he says. In picking the movers, he acts almost completely on impulse, feel, that ache in your stomach that you've got a good one. When one quotes somber maxims from the fund's annual report ("Before Winfield invests in the securities of a company, many factors must be considered. For example . . ."), he just smiles.

Practically his only general operating procedures are, first, that he tries to concentrate his portfolio on about seventy-five issues and, second, that he likes, as much as possible, to stay in companies with fairly large capitalizations so that he has ease and flexibility in getting in and out.

In 1967, Winfield's success was based on Meid's feeling that the in-phase groups would be the computers and the conglomerates, or "deal companies" as he calls them. He was in both early. He bought Control Data, which he calls "the key market story" of that year, at around 38—"the time when everyone was trying to figure whether the computers were a valid play"—and eventually sold at about 140, close to the high. He bought Teledyne at 70 and sold at 220. He got Ling-Temco-Vought at 50 and unloaded it between 200 and 220. "It just seemed to me these companies were extremely cheap and had good entrepreneurial managements," he says.

Meid was also "bagged" several times: Riker Video, an electronics firm which was supposed to be moving big into education, sagged badly; Gulf & Western stagnated; Western Union's big story—a takeover—never came off. Yet he was out of most of these situations before the weaknesses became too prounounced. He was stuck, however, with a small position in the deficit-plagued Cameo Parkway Records, although he had just about written it off.

In 1968, Meid hit far fewer fads and was bagged much more often, and, typically, he is frank in explaining why. "I tend to be a player of trends, and I like to be where the action is," he says, "but last year's market was an up and down market with very few trends. And what trends there were, we simply missed. Take the franchise group. A lot of guys told me about them, but they were mostly a lot of little OTC companies, and I just didn't pay enough attention to them. And I should have been a lot heavier in the financial stocks—the banks and the insurance companies—and the construction stocks. If we had been in them during the first part of the year it would have made the year for us."

The stocks he was in did not do well either. "All those conglomerates we were in in 1967 hurt us in '68, even though we got out pretty fast. We were really hurt, for example, when U.S. Industries got knocked down when they were forced to report residual earnings. One trend I did recognize was the savings and loans, but by the time I got in, the group had topped out.

"What we found out last year was that when you've made it one year, you feel a hell of a lot of pressure the next, and somehow it is much harder to repeat your success."

That David Meid should have an abiding passion of any kind does not seem very likely at first glance. He has a large, wide, face that would appear much more accommodating to a lazy smile than to any more profound expression. His broad shoulders, blond hair and stocky, solid build make you quickly picture him swaggering in chinos and bulky sweater across the campus of a Midwestern state university.

Actually he grew up on a "little ragtag farm" just outside Fort Wayne, Indiana. His father sold insurance and, as soon as he was old enough, David was raising crops and live-stock. When he was fourteen, he borrowed $3,000 from his father to raise hogs, and that year his favorite, known as Elmhurst Cutie (he had names for all his animals), won the grand prize at the county fair. The following year, Cutie's son won the prize and brought a record price per pound. He paid his father back. Then, at sixteen, "There was a fast down-swing in the hog market; and I really got killed." Fortunately, there were other angles: He was picking up $50 a week reselling golf balls that were inadvertently knocked onto his property from a nearby course.

But mostly Meid enjoyed farming. "There's nothing more fantastic than looking at a really straight row of corn that you planted yourself," he says. Then he went to De Pauw University in Greencastle and got interested in business management. One summer he worked as a runner for *The Wall Street Journal* in New York, and he became aware that as a capital gains vehicle, Elmhurst Cutie was pallid indeed. In his senior year, he made $3,000 as business manager or treasurer to five campus organizations. After graduation, he went to Indiana University business school and then into the Air Force, which was "pretty frustrating. I just don't work too well as an employee of the system." He didn't work too well out of the system, either. He and another Air Force man spent $14,000 opening up two coin-operated laundromats outside the base. "We really lost our assets," he remembers. "There was just too much competition around. But it was a good lesson for investing in the market. We had put the money in more because we wanted the venture to succeed than because we really thought it would."

In 1961, he went to work as a trainee in the portfolio management department of Smith, Barney in New York, but he soon found it very difficult to adjust to investment by committee, written recommendations, long, thirty-page portfolio analyses and total reliance on internal research. Eventually the manager told him he just didn't fit into the business, and he was sent off to San Francisco as an institutional salesman. He did well, and was beginning to languish into a comfortable existence when he suddenly realized, "I just wasn't doing what I wanted to do. I decided I had to get back to picking stocks."

He went to Winfield—"they seemed like the most imaginative group in town"—and took a sharp salary cut, from $35,000 to $12,000, to manage some of their private accounts. The situation then at Winfield was pretty confused. Winfield, first organized in 1933, had led a varied existence under various names as a closed-end fund, a balanced fund and various kinds of growth funds. In its latest reincarnation it was being managed by Charles Partridge, sixty-seven, one of the West Coast's best-known investment counselors. Partridge had bought the fund (then called the Bowling Green Fund) in 1956, when it had assets of only about $400,000. He had long had the idea of passing it along to his son, a forty-two-year-old broker, who was clearly less than enthusiastic about the idea.

Soon after he arrived, Meid, says H. L. Jamieson, "sensed a real void in the management of the fund and began moving in that direction." Partridge was disturbed about Meid's presumption, especially since he had recently been through a long struggle with the austere young tiger Fred Alger, who eventually quit and went back to New York to form his own firm and make a name for himself managing the Security Equity Fund (see p. 19). A number of heated confrontations ensued, and Meid was nearly fired.

Partridge then started looking around for buyers to take over the fund. Meid went to a friend at Eastman Dillon to search out a partner to join him in a takeover attempt. He was introduced to Bob Hagopian, a thirty-one-year-old New Jerseyan who had been selling funds since he was sixteen, and who was such a hot shot at Eastman Dillon that the firm used to let trainees observe, through a one-way mirror, Hagopian's tactics in closing a sale. Meid raised $250,000, and he and Hagopian made Partridge an offer. The old man refused, then later agreed, on the condition that his friend H. L. Jamieson, a mutual fund manager, salesman, and underwriter for several decades, who happened to be Hagopian's father-in-law, come in as part of the buying group. "He just couldn't bring himself to sell out just to a couple of thirty-year-old kids," says Jamieson. Eventually the buying group, in the fall of 1966, bought 55 per cent of Winfield & Co., Inc., the management company. Meid owns 30 per cent. His net worth is now well into seven figures. (Jamieson is chief executive officer of the fund, but he quite happily lets both Meid, who is president of the management company, and Hagopian run their own shows.)

It was touch-and-go right after the takeover, though. One week the market was badly blasted. "Out of the twenty most active stocks, which were almost all down, we owned about fifteen," Meid recalls. "We were off 16 per cent for the week, and the $14 million we had when we came in was down to $11 million. We all thought it was the end." But the market rallied the next week, and Winfield has been moving upward ever since.

Meid's involvement with the market has been so intense that a number of his associates have been attempting to get him to relax a bit more, and at their urging he recently bought a 26-foot sloop with which he hopes to race. His principal avocation, though, has turned out to be work for the San Francisco ghetto of Hunter's Point. He has recently become increasingly interested in "becoming a part of the community" and in helping those who lack the same opportunities he had. He became a director of the local Boys Club, which included 450 boys from six to sixteen, and succeeded in getting a number of them jobs in San Francisco's financial district. His biggest accomplishment, though, was investing the club's assets in some hot stocks and transforming $7,000 into $85,000, thus making possible a great increase in the club's programs.

"I'm not much at face-to-face work," he says. "It's slow, a whole generation of work, and I'm too impatient. But I feel very strongly that these boys should have a chance to fulfill their potential, and money, even $100, might make some of the difference. So that's one thing I can do. I can make money for them."

Winfield remains his abiding passion, however, and he has been undergoing a stiff self-analysis in an attempt to avoid repetition of 1968's dismal performance record. His chief conclusion, he says, is "that the fund got too big to be run by one person." He has given large chunks of the fund to two other portfolio managers who are allowed to operate with complete independence. "They see things much differently than I," he says. "One of the guys, for instance, is a fundamentalist. He buys and holds. I'm 18 per cent in cash, and they're fully invested. A number of times, we have had big arguments—I'll want to sell, and one of them will want to buy—so we've just made a bookkeeping change."

But Meid, too, is coming to the realization that the smell of a story, that whiff of hot data, is not always enough. "I've been spending much more time on fundamentals," he admits. "Before, I used to rely almost completely on secondary sources, but now I know more of my stocks in detail than I ever did. With the market the way it has been and even the stocks you really like getting killed, you need real conviction to stay with them. But it is these stocks we hope will lead the market back up."

All this may subtract slightly from the immediate ethereal nirvana of a good story. But even Meid will admit that a booming increase in the value of his fund's shares is the best nirvana of all.

FRED ALGER
How to finish first
in the great performance derby

FRED ALGER is a quiet, unassuming, thoughtful-looking man of thirty-four with tousled hair and glasses, who wears nondescript gray suits with fat suspenders and black shoes, who sits most of the day in a tiny office in downtown Manhattan, and who last year made $1 million. He has a battered wooden desk covered with clutter, and a great view of the building's airshaft. Wall decoration consists of Scotch-taped messages. Five other associates and two secretaries are crowded into the premises. There are a few wooden folding-tables littered with paper cups. The rug has coffee stains. There is no stock ticker, no stock-quote machine, no broad tape—only a couple of well-worn slide rules and a blackboard.

Though Fred Alger doesn't look like a star, there is approximately $300 million whose disposition depends on what he happens to feel like at any particular moment. Security Equity Fund, for which Alger's company, Fred Alger & Company, Inc., is research consultant, has during the past four years chalked up an appreciation of over 260 per cent, one of the best in the industry. An associated fund, Security Investment Fund, has outperformed the market every year, for the past six years, despite a high percentage of bonds.

Alger and his associates also advise two funds in Bernard Cornfeld's Fund of Funds complex called FOF Proprietary Fund Ltd., plus ten private corporate accounts. Alger says that, except for Security Investment, all of these accounts invest in similar stocks and have recorded similarly impressive records.

The Security funds are for Alger kind of loss-leaders, for the fees he receives managing them are quite low. But they are a public advertisement of his abilities. This advertisement has attracted other money involving fees much more interesting. The transformation of stardom into remuneration occurs when you get paid extra for performance. From his other accounts, Alger's companies get 1 per cent of the assets (the amount of money in the fund) or, providing he beats the record Standard & Poor's 500 stock average, 10 per cent (5 per cent for FOF) of the total appreciation (how much his fund has gone up) whichever is larger. Thus the better he does, the more money he gets, and there is no upper limit.

Alger is paid this kind of money because in money management today there is a growing feeling that though good, solid, steady, diligent work may be adequate to achieve respectable results, for a heady performance record that leaves the Dow far behind, something more is needed. Talent, Feel, Knack, Sense, Touch. Either you has it or you doesn't.

Talent is not cheap. Men who are paid for simple brain-power are expendable. If they get sick or tired or fired, a replacement is always waiting. The assistant moves up. The bureaucracy inches on. But talent is a one-of-a-kind commodity. No one looks quite like Elizabeth Taylor. No one flashes his teeth quite like Paul Newman. Fred Alger, though possessed of much quiet self-confidence, modestly does not regard himself as the beneficiary of any miraculous gift. "It's not that we're any smarter," he says. "We just work at it, minute by minute, all day long." But he will agree that "if you want to draw the talent, you have to pay for it." Luring stars these days means dangling in front of them a piece of the action. The sight of men in their late twenties hauling in over a million a year (many managers of hedge funds get a straight 20 per cent of the gain) has not exactly provoked joy among more elderly managers of such money as pension funds, who may get a mere $50,000 fee for careful annual nurturing of a $300-million nest egg. Believers in the "dart throwing" theory (i.e., one closes one's eyes, throws darts at a list of stocks and buys those struck by the darts) that denies the efficacy of fund management in general naturally scoff at high performance fees. But most money managers would agree with First National City senior V.P. and University of Rochester endowment fund head H. W. Tripp who says, "If everyone recognizes the risks, then I don't see anything basically wrong with it." Investment counselor John Hartwell, whose views are discussed in another chapter, points out that profit splits of 50–50 between investors and operators have long been a tradition in other venturesome business fields.

Yet nearly everyone sees potential dangers. "If the incentive gets too high," says George Chestnutt, Jr. (see page 247), who runs the American Investors Fund, "you can get a go-for-broke attitude where people feel that if they lose the in-vestors' money, it doesn't hurt them, but if they can double it, they'll get rich." There is the possibility of outright dis-honesty.

Says one member of Alger's staff, "Too high a fee encour-ages such dishonesty as running up the price of a couple of your thin stocks right around the fee date." Since people are stars only as long as they're hot, an atmosphere of in-stability is produced in the business. Says a pension fund manager at a large bank, "It is like a quarterback who gets intercepted nine times in one game. The next game he sits on the bench." Fred Alger, for his part, is too busy throwing passes at the moment to worry much about the bench. In 1967, of the $1.1 million that was paid to his two companies (Alger himself gets a good slice of this figure) about a million dollars was performance money.

Yet Alger, quite atypically from most other stars, tends to regard this latter with a bit of scorn as "swing money"—nice to have but basically froth. "If your brain freezes up for a year and all you've got is a performance cut, you're dead," he says. "It's all too easy-come, easy-go." He has been work-ing with his accounts to raise the minimum guarantee and cut the performance fee. He budgets his office overhead to match only guaranteed income.

Alger's hang-up is that he really doesn't care much about money. True, he has a nine-room Park Avenue apartment, but then he has a wife and three children under eight. His pos-sessions and material desires are as bereft as his office walls. He is really oblivious to the outside world. Every day he plods through the same dull routine, including a subway ride to the office and a BLT sandwich and chocolate ice cream for lunch. His social life is almost nonexistent (a highlight is Wednesday night duplicate bridge). "I still get lost around New York," he says. "I don't think I could tell you the name of one play on Broadway." Excess personal income is all plowed back into Security Equity. He says he never makes investments for himself.

So if it isn't the money, what is it? The thing that makes Fred run is: The Race; Winning; Number One; Beating the other funds. "I would rather be down 60 per cent in a year and be number one than be up 60 per cent and be number ten," he says. "It is perfectly all right to win by a nose." He likes the spectators to know who is winning. One of Bernard Cornfeld's incentive schemes is the monthly circulation of a performance ranking of all the funds in his empire. One month, due to a misprint, Alger's fund was listed as number two instead of number one. Alger immediately flew to Geneva to straighten things out. "We get a little upset if they don't have us right," he explains.

Thus Alger's strategy is dictated not by some higher standard of desirable gains, but by what the other funds are doing. The starting gun sounds January 1. For most of the time the idea, says Alger, is to "stay with the pack. After a while, it becomes clear which funds are in the lead and we get into the stocks that are making the move." This keeps Alger pretty much up front; his talent for market timing allows him to match the pace, though he is usually still just reacting to what the others do.

Chances to win the race come "during those five or six times a year when you have a chance to do something distinctive, to leave the pack, change your portfolio mix, and move ahead." Stocks that will cause him to leave the pack, he says, fall into two broad groups:

1) Companies whose unit-volume growth is much greater than that of the economy as a whole; growth that can translate into earnings either now or sometime in the future. Alger loves things or people who are trying to "create their own fate."

2) Companies which have experienced a "momentous happening" which will result in "multiple play" for the company's stock, an upward revision of its price-to-earnings ratio. He is especially on the lookout for cyclical companies, which for one reason or another may experience the earnings leverage that comes when lots of excess plant capacity is suddenly put to use.

Alger, of course, is sufficiently bright and sufficiently flexible to know that though it may be nice to surround one's buying and selling with an impressive aura of philosophy, what really matters is that the stock you buy goes up, for some reason—it doesn't matter why. And, of course, the purchase of most attractive growth situations could, after some stretching, be justified by the above two points. And if they can't be justified—so what? Alger, for example, launched not long ago into a furious attack on conglomerates. "Conglomerates [companies which have diversified into many unrelated fields] don't contribute to the thinking of any industry," he said flatly. "All you pay for is the fancy creation of earnings and you're not supposed to think about how they are created or what they represent." Fine. But it then turned out that Alger had on occasion sampled several such stocks. Indeed, one of the chief reasons for his good year in 1966 was his buying of Gulf & Western within a point of its low before the other performance types got in. "I didn't like it when I bought it at 19," says Alger. "But I knew it was going up." It later hit 66.

One of Alger's major abilities has been his knack of understanding what the economy is up to. In early 1966, he and his staff noticed the growing multiple spread between basic industry stocks, which were drifting down, and the flyers. The flyers were being propelled even higher by Gerald Tsai's new Manhattan Fund money and similarly oriented funds. With money becoming tighter, Alger foresaw trouble. Before almost anyone else, he started lightening up on his flyers. He also began selling his airlines—then a hot performance favorite—which he correctly predicted would be soon hit by high new equipment costs and an increasing gap between capacity and volume. At one point, near the October market bottom, he was 30 per cent in cash with his Security Equity Fund. Then he began moving back into the market. The only fund that beat his 8.9 per cent gain for the year (against a badly slumping Dow) was New Horizons, which was loaded up with the new technology over-the-counter companies (companies not traded on the two major exchanges) that began getting a big play around December.

Alger says, however, that in 1967 the same kind of strategy "cost us severely and dearly." First off, Alger was slow spotting the speculation that came out of the market bottom. In August, again sensing a disparity of multiples, he sold such favorites as Kalvar and Monogram Industries. He figured that, due to a probable recovery from the mini-recession, the cyclicals and basic industry stocks would move. He bought into such companies as B. F. Goodrich, Boston & Maine, General Electric, and National Airlines. When the flyers stayed aloft and the others stayed on the ground, Alger rejoined the pack. At mid-December Security Equity, even though it was up about 65 per cent, was ignominiously in tenth place.

The reason for Alger's mistakes in 1967 was not simply a misinterpretation of the economy. It was more serious than that: Alger got out of line with the market. He was running, but his heart wasn't in it; and when your heart isn't in it, they are going to take the ball away from you.

To understand his problem, it is necessary to flash back to Fred Alger, eight years old, son of a well-to-do sometime Detroit politician (he ran once for Governor of Michigan, and later was U.S. Ambassador to Belgium). Young Fred liked to invent things. Basically a loner, he spent afternoons and evenings drawing blueprints and making models of such things as vending machines and swept-winged jet airplanes. "Did you know I was the first to make a contour sheet?" he will inquire eagerly. "Then when I was around twelve, I decided that I would become the greatest golfer in the world. I went out on the course, day after day, from 6:30 A.M. to 8 P.M. That's all I did. But I found I was physically uncoordinated. I had no sense of rhythm. My golf peaked when I was fourteen. After that I did nothing."

Later, he drifted into Yale where, he says, "I spent my time sleeping and going to a lot of movies. It was all a vague shuffling around, a dream world, and I don't really remember much about it. I do remember that I was left-handed and I smudged every test so badly no one, including myself, could read it." He managed to summon up enough energy to avoid flunking, but when he graduated in 1956, he "had no plans for the future, had no job interviews, made no applications to grad school." Finally, in response to his father's demands, he went to work for a Detroit brokerage house of which his father was director. "For some reason," he says, "it turned me on. It wasn't the money. I guess I just decided that it was time to go to work."

He found that as an analyst he could apply the same kind of creative approach to problem-solving that he had as a young inventor. "I have a very limited curiosity about things around me," he explains. "But I do have an imaginative ability that allows me to reason very deeply into a problem, and I have a sense of urgency that allows me to concentrate everything on something until I solve it."

Once, thumbing through the A's in Standard & Poor's he came across American Photocopy. It "looked worth investigating." He spent days checking out other copiers, analyzing cost savings, talking to secretaries. "I know this sounds cloying," he says, "and you probably shouldn't print it because it makes me look a little too good, but after a while I came upon a company called Haloid Xerox and . . ."

After periods at several other banks and funds (another research excursion allowed him to devise a highly complex method of predicting prices of cyclical stocks solely through analysis of inventory levels), he was hired by the Winfield funds, where he became a portfolio manager. In a big personnel struggle he tried to take over Winfield because, he says, "I felt I was the smartest person there." Eventually, after much acrimony, peace was restored when Alger left and formed his own company with one account. A piece of the Winfield operation bringing in $8,000 a year was sold to Security Life, which retained Alger.

He threw all his energies into making that account move. "I tried to avoid hot-stocking it with crud," he says. "I wanted to do well with the big companies that everyone owned by buying them at their bottoms." At the end of 1965, after Alger had racked up the industry's highest performance record (a 77.8 per cent appreciation), he had a meeting with Bernard Cornfeld. Two weeks later Cornfeld gave him a $5 million fund. Other accounts flowed in.

And everything went along well until 1967. The trouble was that the best action that year was with the small companies with the wild technological stories. Alger had spent his career making it with solid companies that moved according to the rules. A lover of substance, he was faced with intangibility and irrationality.

"We found that experience gets to be a disability," he says. "We had learned to be thoughtful but we found out that if you're too thoughtful you don't know what's going on. You have to guard against getting fixed ideas, but we simply didn't want to accept any of these new stocks. We couldn't develop a willingness to pay 50 times earnings for stocks whose stories we couldn't believe.

"Mohawk Data was typical of the things that happened to us all year long. When we first saw it at 25 we weren't impressed. It didn't have the technology. It just wasn't a classy kind of stock. So we watched it go to 60 and eventually we accepted it and went in and made a good profit. But it made us terribly nervous. There were a lot of other stocks we never did get in. Look at Victor Comptometer. Four years of flat earnings, and another coming up. But suddenly it goes from 30 to 90. We looked at it all the way up there but there was really nothing there. Those that bought it were plain lucky. This sort of thing was terribly frustrating. It just didn't pay to be a skeptic."

It was especially galling for him, after being lured into a dog, to watch it fall on its face. "Every time you say it was junk when you bought it and it will always be junk again," he says. "But sometimes there's no other way." Yet he is just as upset when one of his carefully chosen potential winners slumps. "I forget the stocks we made money on," he says, "but I remember the disasters. We dwell on them here. We talk about them over and over, trying to figure out why they failed, why they crossed up our ideas. Emotionally it is terribly draining."

Alger did not win in 1968 either. Alger's two public funds, Security Equity and the Security Investment Fund, although both up, did not match their performance in the previous year. Security Equity was up 12 per cent, compared to the 67.8 per cent gain in 1967. "The more aggressive, the traditionally best portfolio managers did poorly last year, which is too bad," he explains. "In 1968, you made money in two places—blue chips and income-type stocks, especially 'letter' stock." (Letter stock is unregistered stock sold to funds at discount by the company; this stock cannot be resold without permission.)

"We've found that the hardest money to make is in blue chips. You don't make money on just multiple expansion of these stocks without a basic change in the economics. Last year it happened. We were 100 per cent right on the market, in cash at the top and fully invested at the bottom, but we didn't buy blue chips or letter stock for our public funds. Also though we picked the right industries we were in the wrong companies. We liked computer leasing and mobile homes. In computer leasing we picked DPI [Data Process-ing, Inc.] which turned out to be the only one to go down. We looked at DPI, Levin Townsend and Leasco and thought they would rank in that order. As it turned out, Leasco came out first, Levin Townsend second and DPI third.

"We were also right in mobile homes. I believe we were the first ones in mobile homes in a big way. Here again we picked Guerdon Industries which was the only one to go down. We talked to management and thought the company had a lot of things going for it. One thing to remember in mobile homes is that the product is not distinctive, just about anybody can make it. We liked Guerdon, for one reason be-cause they were the only one to develop the concept of modular housing. The company had even gotten FHA fi-nancing which was a massive break through in low-cost housing. But, even with this they still went down."

He favors—"for the next few years"—stocks in industries or companies that have not yet come into their own. These include gambling stocks (Parvin Dohrmann, a money loser last year, is his biggest holding among all his accounts); inte-grated circuit stocks (Fairchild Camera); and CATV.

The gambling business, says Alger, has what he calls "layers of growth." Each year, he says, 8 per cent more people go out to Las Vegas, which is a big convention area. "In terms of unit-volume growth, it's growing between 12 per cent and 15 per cent annually. Its potential margin improve-ment is tremendous. Many of the hotels are already raising rates and they could charge more than they are now."

The same is true, he says, of integrated circuits. Fairchild Camera, he points out, is earning nothing right now—rev-enues are about $225 million. It should be earning, on the basis of its revenues, $3 to $4 per share, yet the company actually took a loss last year. Alger is banking on new management to put the company's product's potential rapid unit-volume growth to work. "Companies like this," says Alger, "should be earning 10 per cent on sales."

CATV, Alger continues, has high unit-volume growth without system growth right now. "The industry," he says, "is currently servicing about 10 per cent of its potential in franchise development. If you treat them like a water company, which is not a bad way to treat them, and value each hookup at $400, with the potential of a million hookups, the network could be valued at $400 million in the market now. Between the potential franchise development and the carrying capacity of the cable itself, the industry's earnings growth should be tremendous."

Alger would probably not admit it, but he is slowly coming to the realization that, as a means of applying his talents, merely picking stocks—especially during a time when success is dependent more on luck than skill—is far from ideal. Ever since his days as a young inventor, he has really been interested in figuring out ways to build something solid and permanent—to play a more direct and constructive role. "I would much rather create something myself than interpret a company someone else has created," he says.

Twice in 1968, when stocks Alger owned showed signs of going sour, he refused to unload them. Instead, he spent much time discussing the company's problems with management, and eventually he helped arrange mergers for both companies. His desire to raise his minimum fee guarantee, his incorporation of his firm (which is less personally financially beneficial than a partnership) are both ways to bring stability into his own operation. Recently his company invested some money in Applied Logic, a small privately owned computer software company in Princeton, New Jersey. He has even tried to sell several companies on an ingenious but highly complex method of financing. Says a friend, "Fred could be a helluva creative investment banker if he wanted to."

But in all this activity involving solidity, stability, permanence, logic, rationality, one gets a hint of a fundamental disease—at least in today's market—that may have afflicted Alger. Maybe he simply is getting too old.

He paused for a long time when he was asked about this recently. He leaned back in his chair and sipped some tea from a paper cup, "Perhaps I have peaked out," he said slowly.

But it was only a momentary twinge of doubt. New horizons of investment banking and the development of new companies may come. But for right now he remained confident that the market was simply another problem that, if worked at, could be solved.

"We're giving away 1968," he said. "Right now we're selling the remnants of our fiascos, throwing out everything we're unhappy with, and getting back in shape. We've been spending too much of our time playing catch up and running scared. Now we're going to win."

FRED CARR
Sniffing out emerging growth with the Dirty Dozen

FRED CARR HAS A PROBLEM. He runs this mutual fund by the name of Enterprise Fund, and a lot of people persist in thinking that simply because it probably has consistently had the best performance record in the business in recent years, because it gained 117.5 per cent in 1967 (leading the field), and 44.4 per cent in 1968 (leading the field in funds of its size)—that for these reasons Enterprise is a swinging go-go fund. These people think that simply because Enterprise has made itself famous by specializing in tiny OTC companies with thin capitalizations that nobody ever heard of, that have a way of roaring up like skyrockets and down like punctured balloons—that because of this Enterprise might just be a little on the risky side.

Fred Carr, who is thirty-eight, doesn't agree at all with these beliefs. "Essentially we are traditional, conservative, long-term investors," he says with much conviction. Carr is not exactly suffering. Enterprise has assets of nearly $1 billion. However, Carr is bothered by the impression that his fund is speculative, because he knows that though there are a lot of mutual fund buyers who love to swing, there are many, many more who are wary of spectacular movement in either direction. This is a very important consideration because, as we shall see, Carr is attempting to build not a lean, stripped-down fund for the elite, but a bulging colossus for the masses.

Carr thus does everything possible to engender the impression that Enterprise is as justly deserving of the Rock of Gibraltar trademark as Prudential. He tirelessly spells out, in solemn tones, his traditional, conservative, long-term philosophy—heavy with terms like "emerging growth company" and "risk-reward ratio"—to financial groups. A truly effective show awaits visitors to the Enterprise offices on a few upper floors of the City National Bank Building in downtown Los Angeles. It is a veritable time machine (like Williamsburg and Sturbridge Village), plunging one back several centuries to an era of darkwood paneling, musty smells, libraries with shelves full of dusty financial books; and such accoutrements as an old ladder for reaching the upper tiers, old etchings on the walls, framed verities ("Be not too fond of Honour, Wealth, or Fame, since none of these can beautify the mind"—Emal. Asutin Scripsit, May 18, 1736), a tall grandfather clock and all manner of other cozy memorabilia. (Only the cynic would carp at the lush display of plastic greenery, the miniskirted receptionist, or the complete lack of order to the books which, Carr admits candidly, "we bought by the yard from a Santa Monica book store.") The time-warp is skillfully carried to the interior offices whose ancient trappings all but conceal the stock-quote machines, Dictaphones, Electrowriters, and multibutton telephones. "The decor," Carr says with total seriousness, "fits the personality of our staff."

If all this seems like pretense, it is fortunately the only pretense Carr allows himself—indeed, he seems rather uneasy in dealing with the problem of image. His success is based on his belief that in order to come up with investment ideas that haven't already been milked dry by others, one must studiously avoid being influenced by what everyone else is thinking and doing. Carr has tried to purge from his organization and from himself all traces of emotion, snap judgment, preconception, prejudice—anything that might inhibit cold, dispassionate realism.

Carr's true personality is reflected not so much by his office's antique furniture as by the series of hard-line, minutely controlled Frank Stella op art on his wall. It would be hard to conceive of anyone more distant from the superthyroid gunslinger, atingle with the emotions of the market. He is a quiet, calm, affable man, with a disarmingly open face and a wide, shy grin. He speaks in a soft, polite, slightly high-pitched voice, but mostly he just sits and listens. He seems devoid of the overlays of affectedness which are often thought to constitute presence. "Fred is a completely uncomplicated man," says an associate, "tremendously well-integrated and free of hang-ups. He has himself under superb internal control. He is solid, like granite."

For his portfolio, Carr avoids both the well-respected traditional growth companies which were once thought mandatory for the respectable fund ("you get no special credit for losing money in du Pont") and the high p/e favorites (price/earnings ratio is a stock's price divided by its per share earnings) of the performance funds ("A performance fund manager who is willing to build his portfolio with high-flying, high multiple securities no matter what their intrinsic value is a skier who might look good, but could be out of control. He may make it down the hill without breaking his neck and he may not. This kind of money management is certainly nothing more than an extension of the 'greater fool theory.'") Among the stocks he sold when he took over Enterprise two years ago were a couple of then-popular computer-leasing companies. "I have never been able to conceptualize why a finance company is worth forty-two times earnings," he said. In 1968, Carr did not make even the tiniest dabble in such high-flyers as Control Data, Teledyne, Xerox, Itek, and Polaroid.

Instead, Carr buys "emerging growth companies"—usually small, unrecognized firms with consistently improving earnings, low p/e's and top-quality management. Because of the volatility of these stocks he is generally a slow buyer, often taking weeks or months to build a position. To prevent rumors of "Enterprise is buying," which can quickly shoot a thin stock up 30 per cent or more, he employs an elaborate security system of such devices as code names and numbered brokerage accounts. Carr sets a rough period of time— from eight months to two years—during which the stock should double as other less prescient investors become interested. (Enterprise's 1968 turnover was 76 per cent.) He sees Enterprise as a kind of "wholesaler"—unearthing good buys and then reselling them to such institutions as pension funds and other funds.

A number of admittedly envious mutual fund executives suggest that because Enterprise is a large pool of money chasing small companies it has several advantages over other types of funds. A good part of Carr's success is due to his ability to obtain sizable blocks of the offerings of new issues, many of which quickly double and even triple. "He has incredible contacts with underwriters," says a San Francisco broker. "You'll see he got a huge chunk of, say, Friendly Ice Cream, and you'll wonder how in hell he came up with all that stock. We're one of the biggest houses on the coast, but we'll get only a few hundred shares."

Another advantage that is pointed out is the marked influence that a fund the size of Enterprise can have on the stocks in which it invests. Large, steady buying in a thin issue will almost certainly push up the price and attract new buying from other funds. Conversely, in time of weakness, new buying can help stabilize the price. Explains one fund head, "The question is not can you sell the stock, but can you support it. It's like being a specialist for the stock exchange."

Carr denies that he purposely influences the prices of his stocks by such tactics. But even if he did, he says, it wouldn't do much good. "We buy for the long term, and over the long term nobody can maintain the price of a security if it doesn't have the fundamentals to begin with."

In any event, by the time these stocks are being played with by the real go-go funds, Carr tries to be long gone. "I'm not going to outsmart myself when the multiple starts going up dramatically. In this kind of situation, the risk starts outweighing the reward. We tend to be early sellers, and we have no desire to participate in the last hectic points of a big rise." (Carr will hold many of his favorites despite their high p/e's if he thinks their future growth rate justifies it.)

Many of Enterprise's winners are almost legends. Among his best choices have been the recently hot franchising issues.

"He's really had that field down cold," says an admiring West Coast fund analyst. His best achievement came about two years ago when he provoked some laughter by adding a company called Kentucky Fried Chicken to his portfolio at an adjusted price of $3.50 (fifteen times earnings)—it was $52 by mid-1969 and he is still holding it. He bought Republic Corp. (Republic Studios, Consolidated Film Labs., etc.) at $5 (only five times earnings) and later sold in the low $60's (at a p/e of 33). "I felt the company had the ability to become substantially more profitable on existing assets alone," he said. "But mostly we bought it because of management changes. New people had made Republic a new company." In 1968, Carr more than doubled his money in such companies as Hyatt Corp. of America, an aggressive, financially astute firm with a growing chain of hotels, motels, and coffee shops, and U. S. Financial, a little-known but venturesome organization specializing in title insurance, mortgage financing and home-building. Enterprise has also gone into such unknowns as Kewanee Scientific Corp. (he made 60 per cent), which makes laboratory furniture for schools, and Cellu-Craft, Inc. (he made 100 per cent), a small packaging company.

Carr finds that his three-thousand-mile separation from Wall Street is a distinct advantage. "It keeps us apart from the rumor mill and the contagious vivid feelings about changes in the market," he says. "Ideas streak around very quickly there and it is easy to follow them like sheep. Too many people put their money on word of mouth—word of mouth from someone who probably made up his mind by word of mouth to begin with." Carr pays little attention to the latest chart fads, almost never meets with other fund managers and, in fact, says he never even takes a glance at anyone else's portfolio. He relies instead on fundamentalist research ("With knowledge comes comfort," he says) and, most important, on a uniquely organized seismographic system to pick up the first sounds of small, but bubbling pools of black ink.

This system is staffed by a group of analysts and investment bankers termed enthusiastically by Enterprise officials as "The Dirty Dozen" and "Twelve Angry Analysts." None of these men—who, in fact, number quite a few more than a dozen—are formally employed by Enterprise. (In fact, Carr employs no analysts himself at all. "Why should I have somebody here analyzing entertainment stocks when I can pick up the phone and talk to the number-one entertainment analyst in the country?" he asks.)

The Dirty Dozen-types, says Carr, are generally "relatively young—in their late twenties or early thirties—bright, intense guys, usually loners who are frustrated by the investment committee process. I don't think they would work very well together." They are men, says one Enterprise officer, who "look for plays, not coverage. They may not know a hell of a lot about IBM because they know ten other analysts do, but they're up-to-the-minute on Scientific Data Systems. They're always traveling around out on the hustings, asking executives about which of their competitors is the toughest, what they're buying for their own portfolios. They're dropping in on trade shows looking for interesting gadgets, chatting with company reps. Even at a party, they've got one ear cocked for a hook into something. They may call you only two or three times a year, but when they do it's well worth listening. The only problem is that if they're really good they outgrow you very quickly, and soon they're managing their own funds. We try to find young guys, a year or two out of school who are still hungry and fresh."

The reason these people are anxious to give Carr that all-important first call (allowing Carr to get in before others push up the price) is partly because of the massive brokerage business Enterprise commands—like most funds Carr rewards helpful brokerage houses with commission business on his portfolio transactions. Also important, though, is Carr's willingness to listen to practically anyone pitch anything, and to give a quick response. It is obvious to Carr that many of the most attractive situations are attractive because others have dismissed them as silly or unimportant.

"When I used to be an analyst," says Carr, "I would often go with ideas to Eastern funds and after quite a while I would get some second-level man who would say ah-h-h-h, well, thank you very much and that would be it. You've got to be responsive to these guys. You've got to say yes or say no, and tell them why if the answer is no."

"It's terribly easy to interject roadblocks when somebody is trying to tell you something," says an associate. "Everyone in this business has a strong ego, and there is a tendency to leap up and interject yourself prematurely. You either try to tear the guy's story apart before he's told it or you sit there, fold your hands, stare skeptically and command the guy to talk as if he were a circus act. It's a little like reviewing a movie; you have to suspend your disbelief until the picture is over or you can miss the whole point. But the main thing is to show some respect for the other guy. Fred will sit there and politely listen, even to some obvious screwball from out of the blue, long after other people would have blown their top and thrown the guy out."

The unconventional operation of Enterprise has, not surprisingly, produced a large amount of criticism. "The recent
market atmosphere for funds like Enterprise has been perfect," says the head of a management company that advises
several conservative funds. "But he's never been through a
period like 1962 when many secondary companies took a real
bath and never recovered." He goes on to point out that even
though Enterprise did relatively well in the recent sluggish
market (the small growth companies, especially those with
new issues, continued to boom) this situation will not last
indefinitely. Indeed, Enterprise through the middle of 1969
slumped badly as the small growth stocks sold down from
their highs, and funds became interested in larger, more conservative companies.

Carr's reliance on outside expertise, though more and more
today's vogue, is viewed by many as potentially dangerous.
"In constantly trying to plug new people into the system you
lose consistency, control, and continuity of coverage," says
Robert G. Egelston, head of rival Capital Research Company,
which has a stable of in-house analysts. "And though brokerage research is strong during aggressive upmarkets, I question how good this pool of outside experts will be during a
period of less economic expansion and the probable new era
of lower commission rates."

But the most serious questions about Enterprise concern
its swiftly growing size. How can a huge fund continue to
prosper by dealing in tiny, thinly held companies? How can
it acquire any meaningful piece of a company that trades in
only a couple of hundred shares a day? How can it avoid
running into the seemingly immutable law that as a fund's
size increases, its performance declines?

Carr, of course, quickly dismisses most of these criticisms.

He sees his hopefully prejudiceless system as extremely adaptable to changes in the market. Whatever happens, value will always be value. "I really see ourselves as running a defensive fund more than anything else," he says, and even in the worst markets, he feels, the growing, well-run, low-priced company is the best bet. It is also protection for his whole system and the "too goddam many mistakes that we make."

Carr thinks, further, that there is an almost unlimited supply of emerging growth companies around (in the first six months of 1968, Enterprise established positions in 177 new companies), and that the larger Enterprise becomes, the more opportunities come its way. The dollar amount invested per company is remaining fairly constant. The only problem in getting bigger is "not size itself but people." The problem with many large funds, he points out, is that they became too large to be managed by the traditional system of having one manager in charge of the entire portfolio. Last year, Carr, in a move that has caught on at many other large funds, divided up his fund into five sections and gave the slices—perhaps fifty stocks—to separate portfolio managers. Nobody specializes in any particular industry—"We don't believe in the industry approach," Carr says—and the different sections are meant to act virtually like independent funds. He sees no limit to almost unending expansion, maybe even to $25 billion with, say, seventy-five portfolio managers. "It is only a question," he says, "of getting portfolio managers with enough talent."

Such an empire would fulfill a dream Carr has had since childhood. Carr's father, who emigrated from Rumania at the age of ten, owned a small fruit and vegetable market near their home on the outskirts of Watts. Carr was deeply impressed that "though he worked six and seven days a week and even made what you'd consider a comfortable living, he was never really able to accumulate anything, to put something away for the future." In high school, Carr used to invest in the market with money he earned from paper routes and other jobs. "I would buy little speculative things," he remembers, "and I would invariably lose. I just didn't know what I was doing."

During those three years at City College of Los Angeles and LA State (where he studied finance and advertising), he gradually developed the goal of "putting together some sort of stake, something I could build up." After leaving the Army in 1953, he decided against returning to school ("I thought it would be a waste of time," he says), and instead partnered in several businesses—pouring concrete driveways, running service stations, speculating in real estate— with a friend with whom he shared a small apartment on Manhattan Beach.

By 1957, when he was twenty-six, he had put together $10,000 and he decided to become a broker's assistant at Bache. There, he began to perceive what the munificent results of good research could be. With typical plodding, arduous thoroughness, he would dig into companies, "really taking them apart to see what made them tick." "In retrospect," he admits, "I think I spent too much time on each individual company. There is a point you reach when there just isn't any sense knowing more. Information that the janitor takes home a few pads of paper every week, for example, is sometimes interesting to know but it has a zero investment value."

Carr became well-known to his superiors because he would often spot errors in Bache's research reports, and he advanced rapidly. He moved to Ira Haupt (until the firm was sunk by the 1963 salad oil scandal) and then to the aggressive Beverly Hills brokerage firm of Kleiner, Bell & Co., as director of research. It was during this period that he developed the emerging-growth-company philosophy. "I guess it was based on all the money I'd lost in the market back in high school. Buying low-multiple companies helps you minimize the impact of your mistakes."

This also happened to be the philosophy of a man named Douglas Fletcher, who ran several modest growth funds. Fletcher was looking for a man to manage the California Fund, a small fund with assets under $21 million investing only in California securities which, despite its rather respectable record, Fletcher wanted to move into other fields. Fletcher was impressed by Carr, who often had called him with investment suggestions. "He was a very bright person, with an independent, entrepreneurial-type mind, the kind of person that might go out and start his own business," says Fletcher. "And he didn't have any preconceived notions about running a mutual fund." Carr joined Fletcher in the fall of 1966. "A lot of my friends thought it was a stupid move," says Carr—it meant a salary cut from $100,000 a year to $40,000—but "I saw an opportunity to help build a business and to create a quality product instead of just making a lot of money every year."

It has proved to be a sage decision. Carr's equity in Shareholders Capital Corp., a holding company that owns the management company for the eight current or soon-to-be-established Fletcher funds, is currently 877,000 shares (he bought a 20 per cent interest when he joined for $200,000). Shareholders Capital, which manages $1.7 billion in assets, has joined the growing group of fund management companies to go public, by selling a million of its shares (of the 6.2 million outstanding) at $20 a share (about twenty times estimated 1968 earnings); by the middle of 1969 it had risen to $40 a share. This is a rather high multiple for an emerging growth company—most management companies sell at a p/e of around 12. Fletcher does not plan to allow the company to sit around paying dividends like some of the others. "We're going to run it in a different manner," he says. "The officers for most of the other companies sold their own stock, but we're selling all new stock so there is no situation of a bail-out. We anticipate an aggressive expansion program," which, said the prospectus, may be "into businesses not necessarily related" to Shareholders Capital's present business. Already SCC has acquired a Los Angeles package of apartment house investments. In order to get approval of the prospectus from the SEC, the company did have to give up being advisor for two of Bernard Cornfeld's Fund-of-Funds funds: the $65 million Douglas Fund and the $17 million Carr Fund. The SEC reportedly was not happy to see earnings from Cornfeld's empire, which the SEC banished from the United States, show up in a public company in the United States. In any event, considering Carr's Shareholders Capital stock, his roughly $1 million in Enterprise Fund shares and those of other SCC funds, and some scattered real estate, his net worth should be well over $35 million.

As one might expect, Carr has been much too busy helping his stake grow to translate much of it into material possessions. He, his short, slender, blond wife Dianne (whom he met when she was working in the new accounts department of a bank), and their three young children live in a comfortable but unostentatious house on a palm-tree shaded street just off Wilshire Boulevard in Beverly Hills. He commutes daily in his Jaguar sedan and spends his evenings poring over mounds of material from the daily SEC reports to *Advertising Age* ("It gives you a good idea of what the people are going to be asked to buy six or eight months from now.")

Perhaps his only avocation is an energetic physical self-improvement campaign. He has been developing into a health food and exercise addict. He tries to play handball three times a week, pores over exercise books, and regularly goes to such health food centers as the Aware Inn on Sunset Strip.

Actually, Fred Carr almost seems to regard himself as a self-contained, emerging-growth company. Though most people would regard the accumulation of $35 million as an excuse to slack off a bit, Carr acts, in fact, as if he were still back pouring concrete driveways. Indeed, his eyes actually light up as he discusses the necessity, on the West Coast, of being up and moving before the seven A.M. market opening. "I love it," he says with considerable gusto, as if jumping out of bed in the morning were one of life's transcendent delights. "It gives you a great shot at a full, full day."

COE SCRUGGS
Turning the ambush
into an investment strategy

"THE REAL REWARDS in finance are the esthetic ones," says Leonard Coe Scruggs, "especially if you're an intellectual ruffian like I am."

Scruggs has used two words which epitomize his idea of money management: *esthetic*, in that to achieve true fulfillment one must rise above the idea of simple capital accumulation; *intellectual*, in that to reach such heights, to produce a Pollack instead of mere chicken scratchings, one must be capable of a much higher order of conceptualization than that practiced by most money managers.

The art, or whatever you want to call it, of investing is actually, of course, a very simple thing: the selection of stocks that will go up. If encumbering this process with a soaring and not very comprehensible overlay of rhetoric does not always seem especially relevant, one should not hold this against Scruggs, for it makes him a much more interesting and engaging individual than the average money manager.

Coe Scruggs, who is forty, is managing partner of Scruggs & Company, a small ($13 mllion) hedge fund (see page 112) which he started in February 1968 and which is permitted to employ a wide variety of devices not allowed regular funds —including selling short, borrowing money and investing in commodities—in an attempt to appreciate its assets. More and more such funds have become the logical destination for men like Scruggs who feel they are blessed with superior investment talents, who desire to give these talents the most free, least fettered rein and who enjoy matching wits (the relative net asset values are published daily) with others of similar inclination.

In his Wall Street office, Scruggs affects a somewhat para-doxical air of austere aloofness and homey informality. It is shabby and cluttered and Scruggs and his partner Mike Ep-stein sit jacketless with rumpled shirts, and smoke big fat cigars, their suit jackets dumped on doorknobs. Scruggs is a big man with a large, round face, brown eyes behind horn-rimmed glasses, and prematurely graying, almost white, hair. He speaks with an only slightly rectified drawl. One is led to the assumption that Scruggs' personality and feelings are as casually strewn about and accessible as the more tangible office accoutrements. The opposite is the case. Questions about his private, personal thoughts bring monosyllabic an-swers, while questions about the market, the economy, the meaning of history, the existence of God and other pressing matters elicit a chuckle—"it is fortunate for you that you asked me"—and then a torrent of intellectually agile philos-ophies, delightfully spiced with calculated heresies.

One of his favorite, though relatively mundane, topics is

what he likes to call "the permanent institutionalized rot of American currency." This rot exists, he says, because "we have irrevocably embraced social priorities—the elimination of racial problems, poverty, and even fluctuations in the business cycle which used to correct inflations—which are being underwritten by the monetary authorities. The result is that bad news is as bullish as good news. For as bad news comes, the government pumps money into that segment of the economy needing it. Thus we have continuous inflation, 5 and 6 per cent a year." Riskiness in investing is banished, businessmen are protected and everyone, he maintains, is conditioned "to cash in on a sure thing."

The smart investors come to realize, he goes on, that "as long as money has cancer, there is no viable alternative to equities. The bond market is dead. Bonds are for chumps, suckers. Soon triple A's will be marketed to yield 8 per cent, and it will be difficult to sell them without some equity kicker."

"Fortunately for our economic health," he asserts, his eyes assuming that especially mischievous sparkle reserved for particularly pithy aphorisms, "we in the U.S. have taken the Protestant ethic to its logical extreme in that we have made a sacrament of money. [Scruggs, as we have seen, excludes himself from this development.] People seek money not for its enjoyability but for its symbolic value. Money is considered to be an end in itself, and as long as this belief continues we will have a profitable economy."

How is that? one asks, with the distinct feeling of playing the inferior role in a Socratic dialogue.

"While in other places people work to make money so that they don't have to work, in the U.S. it is the people with the most money who work the hardest. If the upper classes instead valued, say, culture, then the lower classes would have to work much harder. In exchange for the cultural impoverishment of the upper classes you have the material comfort of the lower classes, and a perpetually strong economy."

To focus more precisely on Scruggs' view of investing, one must refer again to another word in that first sentence: *ruffian*. Scruggs doesn't use it in the brutal bullying sense, but just to mean someone who dispenses with others' laws and rules and creates his own. He tends to believe in Jack Dreyfus' famous dicta that one should avoid stocks everyone is bullish about since everyone is probably fully invested in these stocks and there is no one left to buy and push the price further upward; and conversely that one should concentrate on stocks everyone is bearish about since there is a maximum chance they will go up.

Scruggs developed his investment ideas while he was financial vice-president and manager of the portfolio for American General Life Insurance Co., a huge $1.5 billion insurance complex which included five life and seven fire and casualty companies, and substantial minority holdings in four other insurance companies. Scruggs managed nearly half a billion dollars of the company's stock and bond holdings. In an interview while he was at American General he advocated purchase of what he called "formula stocks": stocks which are "fine pieces of merchandise which happen to be out of fashion. There is probably a good reason for this but it will have been overdone. A likely candidate would be a leader in its industry which has sold off badly and is just sitting there and doing nothing because everyone will be able to cite a litany of ten reasons why it should be sold, and it will probably be selling at bargain prices. If we buy it, this means we are going against the Street's judgment which incidentally is a lot different from the performance fund man who looks for something fashionable he can get in and out of. Timing is important because you obviously don't want to rope a calf when it's going downhill. Still, since they're mostly sold out when I buy them, our vehicles have minimum risk.

"All this time I'm looking ahead about six months when the performance guys will start to want to play with them at higher prices. It's like the military tactic of the ambush. Like the Viet Cong, I try to figure out where they'll be six months from now." He remembers specifically getting into the sulphur stocks in 1963, and the savings and loans and the building materials issues in 1966—all months before they became fashionable. "But as soon as the performance boys get in, you've got to get out. They bring so much speculation, so much publicity, so much abuse, that to survive their attention, a stock has to be a super stock, like Xerox.

"Timing on the buy side doesn't have to be too precise, and you can buy the good ones at your leisure. You may be a little off, but you'll still get 5 to 7 per cent. It's like your wine cellar. Even when you aren't drinking it, you're still gaining value. But selling is another matter. Take the building materials situation. It took the performance guys with their charts weeks longer to see that the building boom was aborting as the long-term interest rate decline halted. We had bought things like U.S. Gypsum and First Charter in September and October of 1966 and we were out by summer. In June they were still trying to get out, when those stocks were off 20–30 per cent from their highs. The essence of selling is again like that of an ambush: hit and run."

In deciding which groups to purchase, Scruggs avoided

one form of artistry he calls "portfolio esthetics." "We don't go along with any of this stuff that says so much of your money in this group and so much in that. We have no sacred cows. Everyone is a candidate for the abattoir."

While at American General, he also became involved in what he called "some fun things over in the bond market." Most institutions tend to avoid anything rated below Baa, but Scruggs typically broke tradition by going after Ba bonds. (Bonds are rated AAA and downward, depending on the degree of risk.) "These whorehouse bonds are a vast junk-yard of colossal opportunities, if you look at them. Consider the busted convertibles [bonds whose convertibility feature, due to a sharp decline in the common stock, is considered to be worthless], which are usually rated Ba. Long after they are issued and the once-hot stock begins to cool, the convertible feature is no longer of interest to the market. The speculators don't care about the convertibility and the institutions won't touch them because of their rating. So they sell low, yield high and carry the apparently useless convertibility feature." But often the company's fortunes will come back to life and infuse the converts with a fresh bit of glamor. "Look what happened with our KLM converts. When we bought them they were freely available in the low 80's. Yielding 6½ per cent. Very high at the time when called, they sold about 150 and even more if the stock was held. This is a way of putting bonds into the portfolio that are dollar-good and have this little time-bomb of convertibility ticking away."

The performance demands of Scruggs' hedge fund are such that he no longer can afford to play the bond market—the payoff time is usually too long—but the *main* thrust of his investment philosophy has remained unchanged. He still scoffs at "the performance guys" and likes to buy not the hot stocks

but undervalued issues with good fundamentals with the ex-
pectation that "lightning could strike any time." He hopes
that "the good news will come in a year" and likes to have a
stock pay off by doubling or at least moving up 50 per cent
within six months to a year. His idea of short-selling is similar
to that of going long ("Buying long" is simply buying a stock
with the hope it will go up. "Selling short" is borrowing stock
from someone and then selling it, with the hope that the
stock's price will drop and you will later be able to buy back
shares to repay the loan at a lower price. See page 114.)
Rather than search out a "heart attack" at which everyone
jumps at around the same time, he looks for "a case of cancer" which, though generally undiagnosed, will become more
apparent as the disease spreads—he cites recent illnesses in
television and sulphur stocks. Ideally he would like to concentrate on fewer than ten issues, but he says that recent
markets have "changed colors and directions" so much that
he has been in 30 or 40 stocks at one time and his turnover
has been much higher than it would have been if "I had been
able to sense a steady market direction."

In 1968, Scruggs did especially well in gold stocks, several
salt companies and the cocoa market where "we made a killing." For the next three to five years, he sees a return to such
old-line blue chips as GE, Kimberly Clark, Caterpillar, Scott
Paper and the salt stocks "which have been out of favor
since 1961 but by the time you publish this will probably be
overpriced."

Coe Scruggs' father and grandfather were both stock-
brokers, in Fort Worth, Dallas and Oklahoma City; but
though it may seem that he arrived at his current occupation
by a smooth, neat path, in reality the route was more tortuous.

He grew up in Mineral Wells, Texas, and remembers at the

age of fourteen chalking prices on the board of his father's securities office. Later, somewhat eclectically, he spent six years in three universities studying economics and a wide variety of such other subjects as Mexican church architecture, before receiving a bachelor's degree from New York University in 1949. Then he went after a master's at the University of Texas before the Army drafted him in 1952. Advancing to lieutenant, he was assigned to demolitions at Fort Hood but he kept up on finance: "By the time *The Wall Street Journal* arrived at eleven in the morning, I had everything else taken care of."

He spent hours poring over financial journals, and one day he noticed a study comparing the then vastly undervalued shares of Royal Dutch Shell with those of Jersey Standard, which were having a boom. Scruggs figured if the big international oil companies were so undervalued, the little ones would be even more so. By statistical analysis, he spotted several small British outfits which, he decided, could actually be bought on the London stock exchange for less than their net cash, which meant that whatever oil wells they held would, in effect, be purchased for nothing.

After leaving the Army in 1955, he flew to Trinidad for a month, where these companies were based, to check out his hypothesis. Then he went back to Texas to find backers for a big takeover operation. But the memory of the 1938 expropriation of foreign-owned oil properties by the Mexican government was still in peoples' minds, and he was turned down. "I was a year too soon," he recalls. "Foreign oils weren't fashionable yet."

Finally, in New York he was able to interest a man named Joe Gruss, of Gruss & Co., a stock exchange member firm which largely invests in lock-ups. (Lock-ups are companies that are expected to be liquidated, hopefully yielding more money per share than the stock's current market price.) With Gruss' capital, Scruggs set about getting control of something called Premier Consolidated Oilfields Ltd., "an amalgam of marginal companies that had been badly used in the past." After a prolonged proxy fight that carried him on frequent triangular journeys between New York, London and Trinidad, he finally won control in 1958. The move paid off so well that Scruggs, at the age of twenty-nine, decided to withdraw from finance and become a university professor.

He soon discovered, however, that the academic pace at the University of Texas was much too slow for him, and he returned to business. "It was a useful time," he says. "I learned that what I liked most is to make things happen, and that finance is the one area of intellectual endeavor where results are always immediately apparent." He became an investment counselor in Austin, then moved to the Dallas brokerage firm of Dewar, Robertson and Dancoast as an institutional salesman. In 1963, he left for the American General job, though it paid only half his previous salary. "I'd never managed a big portfolio before," he explains.

His performance was superlative. His portfolio outperformed the Dow Jones Industrial Average by 100 per cent, and it yielded 50 per cent more in dividends, which is of even greater significance to stockholders, since intercorporate dividends are taxed at an effective rate of 7 per cent, compared with 25 per cent on capital gains.

The main reason for this performance, he says, was the way he was treated by the American General management. "Unlike a lot of insurance men, they were far from hidebound.

They knew what I was and what I wanted to do before I went to work. They ran their company the same way I wanted to run the portfolio: aggressively and unorthodoxly. Unlike mutual companies, management owned 27 per cent of the stock and thus performance of the portfolio was very important."

The top executives left Scruggs almost completely alone and didn't burden him with a lot of collateral duties. "There was no Boy Scout sponsoring, no Junior Chamber of Commerce. American General was not image-minded in the usual sense. We felt if we did our job, the image would take its substance from that." With a small staff of a single assistant and three secretaries, he feels he expended less wasted effort than anyone with a comparable job in this country.

As much as Scruggs enjoyed American General, he was unable to resist when, in 1967, several of his Texas friends offered to put up $10 million for him to begin a hedge fund. He had often condemned his colleagues at the swinging funds—"The performance guys operate on the bigger fool theory and a lot of them will be carried out in baskets," he had once said. But, exercising the true intellectual's duty to shift his theories in the face of changing realities (another example is his now-vehement distaste for bonds), he decided that he could adapt many of his American General ideas to the performance derby, and moreover that he could attempt a lot of things that would have been *verboten* to insurance men. Adds a friend, "Coe was beginning to feel a little too small down in Texas."

One of Scruggs' first acts was to team up with Mike Epstein, then a broker with Bear, Stearns. When Epstein first walked into his office, says Scruggs, "I thought he was a brash Brooklyn Jew. Later I found out he was a talented and brilliant brash Brooklyn Jew." The two men have a very close relationship, yet where Scruggs is often cool and reserved, Epstein is warm and flamboyant.

Adjusting to New York has apparently not been too much of a problem for Scruggs. He, his wife and two children have exchanged an elegant vintage Houston house—complete with Persian rugs, Italian baroque art and a French wine cellar—for a spacious turn-of-the-century mansion in Brooklyn Heights on a promenade on the water, right across from the lower tip of Manhattan. The house served as a location for a Frank Sinatra movie, *The Detective* (only then it was owned by a rich homosexual who had the misfortune of being knifed to death and castrated). Scruggs affects uncharacteristic humility when discussing his diversions: "I ski badly every winter. In the summer I like to swim and sail but I do those badly too." (He has a vacation home on the Jersey shore.)

Adjusting to running a hedge fund has been somewhat more difficult, and his record to date places him somewhere around the middle of the pack. A friend says that psychologically Scruggs has "developed from a double-domed bond investor into an opportunistic 1969-style money manager," but Scruggs readily admits his biggest problem has been acclimating quickly—as any performance fund manager must do—to the rapidly shifting currents of today's stock market. In buying, especially, "Before it didn't matter whether you were six to nine months early. Now it matters very much."

Still, he is thoroughly enjoying himself. "It's great fun," he says. "It's an artistic endeavor, perpetual warfare with no blood. It's a ballot box open five and a half hours a day to register how everyone feels about the way things are going.

And it's a great outlet for just about every personality trait. The elderly can be amused, the aggressive types can flail about however they like and the masochists can beat themselves just as much as they choose." And, he might have added, the intellectuals can relish participating in Great Art.

FRED MATES
The risky ride
of a super-swinger

COUPLE OF YEARS AGO, the quivering ganglia of the
Wall Street rumor-mill picked up signals from a
small company by the name of Magnabond.
Magnabond, according to various sages, had distinguished
itself by developing a truly waterproof paint for swimming
pools, a feat which, when more widely-known, might propel
the stock to some delightfully celestial height. After many investors, both amateurs and professionals, had snapped up
stock, it suddenly appeared that the company's balance
sheet not only had never been audited but, in the opinion of
some, deserved inclusion in *Grimm's Fairy Tales*. Eventually
the company went out of business.

Of all the Magnabond shareholders, only one, a small-
time stockbroker named Frederic S. Mates, who had bought
in for himself and some of his clients, took the trouble to

find out whether the firm's paint held any more water than its financial reports. Mates, in fact, painted the entire inside of his pool with the stuff. "It was really a sad thing," recalls one of Mates' associates. "As the stock went down, the paint peeled off. It was almost as if one were charted against the other." Adds Mates, "Oh God, it was a mess."

It was the kind of fluky disaster that should only happen once to any single intelligent money manager. And that was the way things seemed to be for Fred Mates, who rebounded from Magnabond to form what was for most of 1968 the best-performing mutual fund in the field, by a wide margin. The Mates Fund rocketed from nowhere to rack up, as of December 1968, a spectacular gain of 153.5 per cent. Mates was widely hailed as the new boy wonder, the reigning genius.

Then, abruptly, there arose another Magnabond, only the company's name this time was Omega Equities. Omega Equities had experienced a somewhat checkered career as Tenney Corp., a real estate concern whose shares had once sold as low as 5 cents. After a rechristening in 1967, the company's managers decided to make a then-fashionable conglomerate out of it. Rapid acquisitions were made in such diverse fields as stereo tapes, men's wear and precision equipment. To finance this program, the firm sold "letter stock" to several mutual funds, including Mates. Letter stock is stock that is unregistered with the SEC and cannot be traded publicly—the buyer signs a letter stating he will not sell the stock for a specified period. Since the buyer is thus locked into his commitment, letter stock generally is sold below the market price—Mates, in September 1968, had bought 300,000 shares worth at $3.25 a share, about one third of the current market price.

Fueled by rosy earnings and expansion predictions by the

Omega management (who said among other things that they were "in the process of acquiring control" of Twentieth Century-Fox, Omega soared to $33 bid in the over-the-counter market. Mates, like many holders of letter stock, valued his holdings at market, despite his low purchase price (a practice that has now been largely discontinued because of criticism of the unrealistic "instant performance" this purchase allows). By December, his Omega holdings had expanded to $6.8 million of his $31 million portfolio.

Without warning, the Securities and Exchange Commission in the middle of December banned further trading of Omega, charging that management had released "incomplete and inaccurate information" and had engaged in "deceptive and manipulative conduct." Mates, who was no longer able to determine the value of his fund's shares, asked for and was granted permission by the SEC to stop selling or having to redeem his shares. The net effect was to toss him ignominiously out of the performance derby just two weeks before he would have walked away with the top prize.

It was an ironic twist for a man whose zealous attachment to the companies in which he invests is perhaps unmatched on Wall Street. He once roundly blasted his wife for purchasing a roll of Scotch Tape when at the time he was in a company called Technical Tape which made a competing product. "A lot of people think when you buy a stock you are just buying a number, as if the stock and the company were entirely separate items," he says. "I take the attitude that when I buy the stock, I am really part of the company." He makes frequent moral judgments of a company's activities. He will not buy a company which makes munitions, for example. Last year, he was actively considering purchase of D. H. Baldwin, the well-known piano manufacturer, but abandoned the idea when he discovered that a division of the company produced bomb fuses. "Why should we get involved with that kind of activity?" he asks. "Why should we buy somebody who makes money from killing people? There are plenty of other good companies around." Though a heavy smoker, he will not buy tobacco stock because of the industry's "unethical advertising which tries to seduce young people." He is also an enthusiastic drinker but, though "the problem hasn't come up yet," he guesses he might not buy liquor stocks either.

Conversely, he feels a special urge to invest in companies whose work he considers beneficial to society. He went into Zimmer Homes once, not simply because the firm made mobile homes—one of the Street's more recent enthusiasms—but because they were doing work in modular construction, which could be a solution to the great need for low-cost housing. He bought a large position in Ecological Sciences because it "is in the forefront of the effort to clean up man's environment and straighten out the ecological balance. The company is superbly exciting." Mates feels that ecology is the industry with the greatest growth possibilities over the next few years. (Some of his other investments are more difficult to justify on humanitarian grounds. Not long ago he bought stock in Cinemation Industries, a distributor of so-called "sexploitation" films. Its most recent offering was a Swedish import called *Inga,* an energetic display of nudity, intercourse and masturbation. "I'm against censorship," explains Mates, who went out to sample the movie the day it opened.)

The initial impression given by Fred Mates is quite contrary to that of a zealous altruist. He is short, wiry, and seems like a cross between a highway used-car salesman and an aging (he is thirty-six) member of the Hell's Angels. His face is a mixture of watchful craftiness and karate-chop-at-the-ready toughness. When he walks he has a tendency to thrust back his broad shoulders and swagger. His head is covered by a shaggy hairpiece, while in the back his own hair resumes to fluff out at the collar with fashionable bushyness.

One senses immediately—correctly, it turns out—that though he is not exactly cocky, the man possesses a significant amount of nervy self-confidence. "I really get uptight when one of our situations gets pounded," says an associate, "but it doesn't bother Fred at all. He just sees it as a good time to buy more." A few years back, Mates became interested in a small Canadian mining company which reportedly had just made a big strike, and he decided to pay the company a visit. He figured, however, he might obtain more information from management if he were accompanied by a mining engineer. Riding the subway one afternoon, he spotted a marvelously hirsute, bearded type with sandals, and for a few dollars he recruited the man for the trip north. In the end, Mates never bought the stock, but by all reports the beard performed admirably, emitting profound, if not terribly audible, mutterings as he carefully looked over ore samples.

After one talks with Mates for a while, the humanitarian bent becomes somewhat more plausible. The face and eyes are softer than they appear at first, and he is really a very gracious, polite individual. He likes to give the impression that his fund is more a means for others to make money than for his own financial aggrandizement. In 1968 he began Mates Financial Services, which handles about $25 million in discretionary accounts—accounts which Mates has total authority to manage. (The brochure advertising Mates' service, incidentally, is one of the Street's more engaging documents. Written in a "I am Fred Mates. I make money grow. Do you want your money to grow? Then give me your money" style, it manages in twelve pages to mention Mates' name twenty-eight times.) He deliberately set the minimum at $10,000, one of the lowest around for this type of service. "There is a real social need for this, especially for people with smaller assets," he says. "Too many of the big brokerage houses have other things in mind besides these people's welfare." He tells of one house he knows where salesmen are regularly called in and told to keep their customers in volatile stocks—it doesn't matter whether the stocks go up or down as long as they move, because in either case the client can be quickly switched into another issue.

He and his wife, Barbara, who teaches psychology at Barnard, meanwhile have been conducting a consumer education program for WWRL, a black "soul" radio station. He decided to do this after his black housekeeper proudly told him all about a new TV set she had purchased in Harlem for $300. "She had been led to believe she was really getting a good buy," says Mates. "But we found she could have gotten the same set downtown at Korvette's for $85." Mates is also thinking of setting up a fund, which he would manage at cost, that would be sold only in ghetto areas.

He sees his own office in ideological terms, too. He calls it a kibbutz, or cooperative settlement, and likes to tell friends he is "the only communist on Wall Street," because he pays employees not according to their work but according to their need. He intends, however, to pay year-end bonuses based on performance.

Despite all these political and social overtones, the fact remains that Fred Mates, except for the Omega Equities misfortune, has been running quite a successful mutual fund. The principal reason is a seemingly antithetical combination of character traits, common to many good mutual fund managers: "On one level, Fred has that strain of a true believer," says Stevan Rosenman, vice-president in charge of financial services of the Mates Fund, and a long-time friend, "but on another level he has an ability to think extremely coolly about something." In a few cases, such as Omega Equities, the "true believer" side wins out, but in most cases he is able to obtain both a realistic appraisal and an intuitive perception of a firm's prospects. He is able to spot that almost esthetic combination of circumstances which, when arranged in just the right order, can cause everything suddenly to glow with eye-arresting color.

"Fred will watch a company for a long time, gathering information from all the technical and trade magazines he reads and many other places," says Rosenman. "Then all of a sudden one more piece of information will come in and Fred will announce that at last the company 'smells right,' as he puts it. When he tries to tell you why, you can follow him about 90 per cent of the way but then he leaves you. That last 10 per cent is too subjective. It's the area where artists work."

Mates is a staunch fundamentalist, and in addition to more conventional data, he likes to know all about the personality of the company and its management, its habits, inclinations, its whole raison d'être. Nothing impresses him more than a management with unrepressed energy. "What I want to know is: do they really eat, sleep, and drink their company," he says. "Take Ecological Sciences. Those guys are unbelievable. They work eighteen hours a day, six and seven days a week. If you want them during the weekend, you can almost always reach them at their office. I've never seen such a driven group of men." (Hard work is not everything, though, and Ecological Sciences has recently encountered difficulties making earnings match its ambitions.) He is very attracted by management's intention to grow by acquisition and he quickly moved into a company called Oxford Finance when it acquired a substantial number of receivable portfolios and loan offices.

Mates is concerned also by the impression an organization's top executives will make on other people: "When I visit them I'm not trying to get information as much as I am trying to figure out what the next security analyst to come along will think. I remember one company that I would have bought if it weren't that the chief executive was an unbearable bore. I just couldn't see any analyst in his right mind recommending the stock because he'd know that if his people bought the stock he'd have to maintain a constant liaison with this guy."

Perhaps more than anything, Mates searches for an opportunity, says an associate, "to buy glamor cheap." He fishes among the small, low p/e growth companies with sales of around $10 and $20 million ("It's a lot easier to take a company from $10 million to $100 million than from $100 million to $1 billion") for something that will attract attention: a new product, new management in a situation with underutilized assets, some idea that, though not yet realized, may be realized soon. His greatest successes have come from buying low into the so-called mini-conglomerates and other small acquisition-minded companies.

While, in a sense, it was the urge to buy glamor cheap that attracted him to Omega Equities, most of his other choices have turned out extremely well. A good example is Longchamps, which in addition to being very acquisition-minded, has developed a method for increasing net from its various restaurants. Based on its experience with the Cattleman restaurant, the company found that by actively promoting late breakfasts, early and late lunches, and after-theater dinners, it could greatly increase turnover, keep seats filled throughout the day and make profits rise significantly. The Mates Fund's Longchamps holdings quadrupled.

Another of Mates' favorite companies has been Equity Funding, which got the idea of selling mutual funds and life insurance simultaneously by using fund shares as collateral for a loan to pay insurance premiums. Mates saw the greater commission opportunities would be very attractive to fund salesmen. Since Mates bought the company it has appreciated over 1,000 per cent. Once Mates has made the emotional commitment to buy a company he is extremely reluctant to sell. "I like to buy stocks and then just lock them away," he says. "A lot of people have made a hell of a lot in the market because they were too stupid to sell."

Fred Mates grew up in Brooklyn, where his father was an attorney for a small real estate firm. His original intention was to become a playwright, whose works would perhaps be modeled on those of his idol, William Shakespeare. He went to Erasmus High, then Brooklyn College, where he majored in English Literature. At BC he wrote and had produced a full-length, free-verse contemporary adaptation of Shelley's "The Cenci," a story about an incestuous father whose daughter eventually kills him. His favorite pastime was reading Shakespeare which he enjoyed especially, he says, because of the Bard's understanding of human nature. ("It may seem far-fetched," he says, "but knowing Shakespeare can be a big help in the market. You learn that people are not what they seem, that a man like J. B. Fuqua of Fuqua Industries is not just a simple farm boy from the sticks, but a brilliant market strategist." Mates' position in Fuqua performed handsomely.)

After graduation from college in 1954, Mates got a job teaching at an elementary school while he spent the evenings engaged in a massive effort to produce a contemporary version of *King Lear*. Then he married a girl whom he had first seen performing as Laura in Tennessee Williams' *The Glass Menagerie* in college. The critic for the school paper had vehemently panned her portrayal, mainly, it seems, because she had refused to date him. Though Mates wrote a letter to the paper excoriating the critic, it was not until a year after graduation that he had asked her for a date.

After he got married, Mates had to quit teaching for something that paid more money. His wife was teaching speech pathology at Brooklyn College. He went to the BC placement office to see what was available, and decided to take a job as a cable clerk in a Bache office on Wall Street. The only experience Mates had ever had in the market was some idle purchases of Canadian penny mining stock but "I was desperate," he says. Soon, however, he rose to the status of a customer's man and even managed to get his clients successfully in and out of the then-booming bowling stocks.

In the meantime, Mates had purchased an Isetta—a tiny, three-wheeled, one-cylinder foreign car with a door in the front. "I fell in love with it and I thought a lot of other people would too," he says. He secured a Brooklyn franchise, borrowed some money, and opened up for business. He was in trouble from the start. For one thing, "the Isetta really laid an egg. It was just too underpowered for American drivers." He began selling Czech motorcycles and Japanese motorscooters, unfortunately some two years before the latter became a craze. Running the agency was also proving much harder than he had figured. At one point he had to recruit his wife to attend a special school to learn how to repair the machines. Her notes constituted the office repair manual. "She turned out to be Brooklyn's only lady motorcycle mechanic," he says.

The principal problem, though, was that "I was terribly undercapitalized," Mates reports. The agency lost more and more money. One Sunday morning when he said he wanted to go out and splurge on a couple of bagels, he had the ignominious experience of having his wife tell him they just didn't have enough money.

Just when things looked the most bleak, one of his former clients happened to come into the showroom and tell him that if he ever went back into the brokerage business, Mates could have his entire account, whose commissions might run around $300 a week. Enticed, Mates closed down the agency, auctioned off the assets, and joined Newburger, Loeb. As it turned out, the old client never showed up, but many new ones did. They were especially attracted by a market letter he had begun writing. It consisted of a few hundred words on small growth companies he particularly liked. His choice did exceptionally well. (His personal wealth today is principally made up of positions he took in some of those stocks.)

After working at several houses, in 1963 he joined Spingarn, Heine & Co., which had offered him a salary above and beyond commissions to write his letter for them. Soon circulation was over a thousand, and business was becoming difficult to handle. In late 1966, Mates decided that by starting a mutual fund he could solve several problems: it would be easier to deal with the clientele; by instituting an automatic withdrawal plan, he could satisfy those who desired steady income; by buying shares in the fund himself, he could profit from his stock selections without a potential conflict of interest.

The Mates Fund opened up in July 1967, and by the following month had $700,000 in assets. Performance was good, if not spectacular, and by January 1968 assets had risen to $1.6 million. The fund was really put into the spotlight, though, by its record during the January-March decline. While other funds were generally losing ground, the Mates Fund actually rose a few points. "What made the difference," he explains, "was that everyone else had a wrong conception about the small growth stocks. These companies were killed during the 1962 crash. In '63, '64 and '65 everyone kept selling them to buy blue chips. In '66, they recovered but were then killed again by the money crunch. Finally in 1967 they started to move, many of them going up three and four times. By January, everyone thought they were overvalued, that '68 was to '67 as '62 was to '61. They didn't realize what a low base these stocks had moved up from. Equity Funding, for instance, which had a 50 per cent compound growth rate, was selling at only six times earnings in June of 1967. The big rise in these stocks was simply a return to normalcy."

While everyone else went heavily liquid, Mates, displaying typically nervy confidence, was buying all over the tape, and stayed fully invested and fully leveraged (the fund is permitted to borrow $1 for every $3 in assets.) As soon as the market began recovering, his portfolio took off.

Suddenly the various rating services began to discover and highlight his performance. By May, floods of money were pouring in, sometimes $1.5 million a day and much of it in small amounts around $500. Mates, who had never expected the fund to be anything but a sideline, was so exhilarated that he failed at first to notice that he was rapidly being buried alive in paper. At that time the fund was being run out of a single tiny erstwhile stockroom at Spingarn, with a staff of only Mates, Stevan Rosenman and his wife. As the mountain of mail piled up, Rosenman desperately recruited outside help. Spingarn partners had to help with the filing. Temporaries were so upset by the confusion they burst into tears. "It was incredible," remembers Rosenman. "We'd work all day and all night and no matter how much we tried, we simply weren't able to handle it."

The situation deteriorated to the point where it became impossible to compute the fund's net asset value accurately or figure out what price to charge new shareholders. Orders for shares sat around unopened for days. The possibility arose that small mathematical errors could have compounded themselves to throw everything grossly out of kilter. ("I should have realized from the Isetta experience that I'm not much of an administrator," admits Mates.) Mates was having considerable trouble from Spingarn, too. An old-line conservative firm, it was collectively chagrined to suddenly find itself with a real-life go-go fund thriving away in its very midst. Mates was urged to go liquid or do *something*.

Finally, on June 4, the Mates Fund—then with assets of $17 million, about $15 million of it from the sale of shares—announced it had stopped selling shares. Almost immediately the two-place Spingarn switchboard was jammed with phone calls. Irate letters arrived by the hundreds. "They told us we had some nerve closing down," says Rosenman. "They acted as if we were cheating them out of money somehow, as if Fred had discovered some wonderful money machine and was refusing to share it with anyone." People offered bribes, anything to get in. And $50 million worth of orders had to be returned.

His performance continued to soar during the fall of 1968. The feeling grew on Wall Street that the Mates Fund could not have achieved its performance without some kind of edge. Mates always had had the reputation, rightly or wrongly, of buying some of his favorite stocks more or less in concert with a large circle of friends in other houses, which often had pleasant effects on the stocks' prices. It was pointed out that two days after Mates bought in, one ASE company issued a very bullish earnings report, causing the stock to spurt ahead and, eventually, to triple. Mates was a good friend of one of the firm's directors, and had visited the man shortly before buying the stock. Others felt Mates was using the new money to jack up the price of his already-established positions—the fund at the time was concentrated in a relatively few issues.

As it turned out, his upward evaluation of Omega Equities and a few other letter stock holdings had indeed been responsible for some of his spectacular 1968 performances. After the SEC action on Omega Equities, Mates wrote down his investment in that stock to his $3.25 cost, which actually turned out to be quite close to the $4-a-share price the stock dropped to after the SEC allowed it to resume trading in early 1969. (The company had predicted 1968 earnings would equal $1.25 a share on $206 million in sales. Actual figures turned out to be an operating loss of 50 cents a share on a mere $9.1 million in sales.) But the revaluation of the security had a severe effect on his fund's net asset value, which sank to only slightly over half its December 1968 high. Finally in June, after imposing a number of restrictions on Mates' trading activities, the SEC allowed him to resume selling and redeeming his shares. The settlement did not require Mates to admit any wrongdoing.

Mates' rapid, widely heralded rise to the top, followed by his equally rapid fall, the latter accompanied by rather severe excoriation from Wall Streeters, has been understandably unsettling to him. "It is always nice to see your name on the top of the charts," he said not long ago, "but this rating everyone by weeks or months is really meaningless. It's just a scorecard for a game the fund managers play among themselves. It doesn't have much meaning for investors unless you do it over a long period, maybe five years."

He glanced at the TV tube, in front of his desk, which displays the stock tape, and lit a plastic-tipped cigar. "Anyway it's uncomfortable being on top. It causes a whole mythology about you that you just can't live up to. And it means everyone is around taking pot shots at you. The real satisfaction I get is making money for people, making poor people rich."

The troubles with the SEC did not bother him that much, he said. "I've played it perfectly straight," he maintained. "I sleep at night."

His biggest problem will be in adjusting his investment ideas to the much larger kind of fund which he expects to have now that he is again open for sales. He recently substantially built up his cash to give him maximum flexibility (and allow him to handle an expected flood of redemptions). "You can go either of two ways," he explained. "There is the Jerry Tsai route of concentrating in a small number of large companies and then turning over your portfolio constantly—a strategy which has failed miserably—or the Fred Carr way of buying a big list of small growth stocks. I've always had a little bit of hero worship for Fred—we buy many of the same stocks—and even though I've been rather concentrated up until now, I think I'll go his way."

Mates' personal life, however, has remained largely unaffected by his tumultuous professional life. Like a number of other fund managers who have zoomed rapidly from poverty to wealth, he has not gotten around to adjusting his standard of living. He would still be buying his clothes at S. Klein if some of his associates had not shamed him into raising his sights. Only recently did he stop bringing his lunch in a paper bag. His only two ostentations are a four-year-old Rolls Royce (he had another Rolls before this which, he proudly points out, he actually sold at a profit) and an apartment in the artsy-chic Dakota on West 72nd Street in New York City, which is very convenient for his wife's job. "I don't think Fred is really happy there," says a friend. "Intellectually he knows he can afford it, but somehow he finds it a little sinful."

He has maintained an interest in the theater—he lost a pile of money when, despite a dazzling array of big names, a musical version of Bruce Jay Friedman's *A Mother's Kisses* closed out of town—but Shakespeare, and particularly Mates' adaptation of *King Lear* have suffered from neglect. Recently he was asked if he might eventually return to playwriting.

"I'm really afraid to," he replied. "I can't think of anything harder to do than write. And you might do a bad play and it would be a year before you'd know it. What I'm doing now is really much easier. Sure, we've had some bad problems. But the main advantage in this business is you know very quickly whether you're right or wrong." On this point few money managers can speak as authoritatively as Fred Mates.

THE PIONEERS 2

Introduction

FOR THE STARS TO RIDE HIGH it was first necessary for pioneers to point the way. Three grand old men served as fathers of the new age of money management. One was Jack Dreyfus, perhaps the first performer, who has long since retired from his Dreyfus Fund, with its famous lion logo, and turned it over to *Howard Stein,* herein profiled. Stein has pioneered in his own way by capitalizing on Dreyfus' market theorems and by showing how to turn a small fund into a large empire.

Another grand old man is Edward Johnson, *"Mister Johnson,"* as he is always called with considerable reverence, who devised much of the original philosophy of performance. But Mister Johnson was mainly a conceptualizer, and it took one of his young employees by the name of *Jerry Tsai,* today the country's best known money manager, to show how this philosophy could be put to use. Tsai was perhaps the first of a whole stream of important money managers to move away from tutelage under the masters to make their own success. His aggressive, bold trading techniques at first shocked the financial world, but they are now common practice.

A third grand old man not only devised an important financial idea, but remains its most successful practitioner. He is *A. W. Jones,* originator of the most secretive as well as the most intrepid money management scheme on Wall Street, the hedge fund.

Arnold Bernhard's pioneering is of a different sort. His chief accomplishment has been to show how the information and knowledge upon which the new style of money management is based can be merchandised to the public. Some critics feel his various Value Line advisory services are one part astrology, and two parts stock market theory; but their towering success over their thousands of competitors is undeniable.

JERRY TSAI
The first star's
sudden flame-out

"**W**E REALLY OWE HIM A LOT," says mutual fund manager Fred Alger. "He was a pioneer. He created the idea of intensive money management and showed the way for all of us."

"He was the product of publicity rather than performance," another fund man maintains. "His problem was that he got too caught up in his own legend."

When people on Wall Street talk about Jerry Tsai, it is with that special contemplative, faraway tone used to pronounce final judgments on deposed statesmen and bankrupt empire builders, men who in their era flourished mightily but, when the times changed, were inexorably forced from the scene. Briefly, with a few slow nods of the head, Wall Streeters display some reverence, a little pity, perhaps a touch of cynicism and then go back about their business.

Jerry Tsai was, in many ways, the first true performer, and the techniques of managing money that he developed later became widespread. He was first thrust into the limelight during the 1950s by his aggressive trading of the big new glamor stocks (Xerox, Polaroid, Burroughs). Many people seemed to believe he possessed mystical powers of the Orient (he was born in Shanghai) which somehow allowed him to perceive the future. Stocks about to leap upward apparently emitted tiny signals—slight tremors before the big earthquake—that only he could receive. Rumors that TSAI IS BUYING! and TSAI IS SELLING!—for his Fidelity Capital Fund, part of the Boston Fidelity complex—usually caused a desperate scramble to follow his lead.

The popular press quickly converged on Tsai, elevated him to the status of a genius. They ruminated at length on what might lie behind his "inscrutable" countenance. (Westerners habitually label "inscrutable" anything from the Orient which they cannot instantly understand.) *Newsweek* impassionedly referred to Tsai as "something of a mystery man" who "radiates total cool . . . from the manicured tips of his fingers to the burnished black tops of his slip-on shoes," and remarked with awe on his "blank, impassive—friends actually call it 'inscrutable'—gaze".

Then in 1968, without warning, Jerry Tsai collapsed as the era of the big glamor stocks, upon which his entire market philosophy was based, abruptly ended. While the Dow Jones Industrial Average was up 5 per cent, and many other performance mutual funds were up 30 and 40 per cent, Tsai's Manhattan Fund, which he had started to loud fanfare in 1966 after leaving Fidelity, was actually *down* 7 per cent, the worst record of any of the 310 funds in the Arthur Lipper survey of mutual fund performance. Superman had been confronted with a giant hulk of Kryptonite. Billy Batson, gagged, had been unable to shout SHAZAM! and switch into Captain Marvel. Spider-Man had lost his radioactivity. The star had fallen.

As the year went on, Wall Streeters smirked, mocked, snorted and scoffed. "Jerry must have left all his brains up at Fidelity," they said chortling. The press went searching for another star. Later people all but forgot about him. Jerry Tsai and the Manhattan Fund were still in business, of course, but reporters no longer beseiged his shiny, rosewood-paneled office with the goatskin-covered bar cabinet. Tsai is buying! was no longer whispered in board rooms. Portfolio managers, analysts and brokers no longer tied up his telephone in hopes of obtaining a tiny hint of which way he intended to move next.

Tsai has not been wasting time despairing about his fall from grace, however. He recently pulled off a business coup that few, if any, other fund managers can match. As Fred Alger explains it, "Jerry has now taken things one step further into the future. First he created enough of an image as a performance man to get enormous assets under his management. Now he has translated that into extraordinary capital values for himself." In August of 1968, Tsai sold his Tsai Management & Research Corp. to CNA Financial Corp., a big Chicago-based insurance holding company that is diversifying into many financial fields. At forty, Tsai, who ten years ago was an unknown, relatively impecunious securities analyst, now (along with members of his family) owns CNA stock recently worth about $35 million. And while growing hordes of fund managers are scrabbling like hungry mongrels to beat each other out in the performance sweepstakes, Tsai has all but withdrawn from the running of the Manhattan

Fund and embarked on a whole new career developing non-insurance acquisitions for CNA.

It should be understood that Tsai is really quite unlike the image the press built for him. He is eminently scrutable. His principal talent is not so much picking stocks but a very Western flair for corporate maneuvering. He has an abiding, also very Western ambition to build up and control any organization of which he is a part. His gaze, furthermore, is not blank but rather animated and, when the occasion warrants, stern and cutting. He laughs easily, and is quite personable and expansive among friends. Not long ago he attended a dinner party and was seated next to a chatty, middle-aged matron. Tsai and the woman conversed amiably through the appetizer and the main course, and as they were eating dessert, she turned to Tsai and remarked, "You know, Mr. Tsai, I'm really very disappointed." "What do you mean?" he replied. "Well," she continued. "everyone told me how mysterious you were. But you're just like everyone else."

Tsai is far from cool—indeed perhaps his chief weakness is an abiding, often tempestuous, thoroughly non-Oriental impatience, and an ardent desire for instant results. At night he falls asleep almost immediately, then often awakens at 2 A.M., his mind so full of ideas about the coming day that he is unable to get back to sleep. Almost all of his spare time is spent plowing through an attaché case which is always filled with brokerage reports and other material.

That Tsai should display so many idiosyncracies familiar to Westerners is not really surprising. Though he spent the first seventeen years of his life in Shanghai, his father was a graduate of the University of Michigan who had been sent back to Shanghai as a district manager for the Ford Motor

Co. During much of the Second World War, however, his father was cut off from the rest of the family in Chungking, and the greatest formative influence on Jerry was his mother, or more specifically, her financial savvy.

"My mother is a very smart lady," he says. "She was always buying and selling real estate, gold bars, stocks, even cotton." One reason he and his sister rooted for her was because whenever these transactions turned out well, they received extra allowances. On her advice, Jerry from the time he was eleven would exchange his Chinese allowance for American dollars to protect his savings from the ruinous inflation that beset China during this period. "Even a movie ticket got to cost $12,000," he recalls. "Every three months, we would have to turn in our old currency for a new issue." Very early in his life, Jerry began developing a strong desire to make it big on the fabled American Wall Street. "What more exciting thing is there for a man?" he asks, shrugging his shoulders. He applied to and was accepted by Wesleyan College in Middletown, Conn., and in 1947, at the age of seventeen, he arrived in the United States for the first time.

Soon he transferred to Boston University where he majored in economics, began trading in the stock market, and graduated in 1949. Only two months later, he picked up his M.A. After a year at a Providence textile company, he returned to B.U. to work on an M.B.A. However, he soon became impatient to move on to Wall Street and got himself hired by Bache as a junior securities analyst. A year later, a friend at Scudder, Stevens arranged an interview with Edward C. Johnson, the fabled "Mr. Johnson" of Fidelity Management and Research in Boston. Johnson thought about Tsai for a month, then hired him as an analyst. Tsai swiftly assimilated the intricacies of money management, and within six years he was allowed to start the Fidelity Capital Fund, Fidelity's first public growth fund.

The idea of performance probably originated with Edward C. Johnson, head of Fidelity (see next chapter). Yet despite this fact, and the fact that Fidelity Trend, Fidelity's other big growth fund, actually outperformed Capital during this period, still Tsai personally received most of the public and professional acclaim. One reason was his race, which created instant allure—the "inscrutable" legend. Another was the retiring publicity-shy nature of both Mr. Johnson and his son, Ned, who ran Trend. Finally, there was the dramatic way in which Tsai operated.

Tsai's specialty was the big glamor stocks such as Xerox and Polaroid, which generally had been considered to be too speculative for anyone but private traders. At a time when broad diversification was the prevailing philosophy, Tsai concentrated his portfolio in a small handful of these glamor issues. Though all responsible money managers bought on fundamentals, Tsai freely admitted he traded by the charts. He would establish positions with dramatic snatches of tens of thousands of shares. Then, watching the technical progress of his holdings very carefully, he would dump his positions with equal suddenness when a company developed tinges of weakness. "I never fight the tape," he said. His annual turnover generally exceeded 100 per cent, an almost scandalous level, then unparalleled among other institutions.

Many on Wall Street were entranced by such flashy maneuverings, but those forced to execute his orders were less thrilled. "Jerry used real bludgeon tactics in his trading," recalls a friend. "He would call up Bache, for example, and tell them he had 100,000 shares he wanted out of no more than two points under the market. If they screamed too loudly, Jerry would just cut back on the business they received for the next month. He knew how to play his leverage." Tsai was almost "sadistic," says a former associate, in the way he cheerfully sent specialists into a state of near collapse on the floor of the exchanges.

The investment climate of the early 1960's was perfect for Tsai. As more and more institutions discovered the virtues of growth and performance, they went searching for the same glamor issues Tsai was buying. Tsai's reputation gave many of his portfolio maneuvers a certain self-fulfillment. His progress within the Fidelity organization, though, had run into a snag. By 1963, Tsai owned nearly 20 per cent of Fidelity Management and Research (Mr. Johnson held 40 per cent) and Tsai clearly expected that after an appropriate period of time he would be running the company. Indeed, those who were at Fidelity say his political activities, though less flashy, were just as adroit as those in the market. But it became more and more obvious that Tsai had a formidable competitor for the top job after Mr. Johnson retired: Ned, Mr. Johnson's son. In 1965, Tsai confronted Mr. Johnson with the issue: was Ned or he to be the successor? Mr. Johnson replied that after all Ned was his son and that it was his intention that Ned eventually take over. As much as he admired Mr. Johnson, Tsai felt he had no other choice but to leave. "Fidelity is a family business and Mr. Johnson's wishes were very understandable," says Tsai. "But I wanted to be number one, not number two." Tsai sold his Fidelity stock back to the company at its book value—$2.2 million or 1.3 times earnings—and set out on his own.

As Tsai worked to organize the Manhattan Fund in the

latter part of that year, the degree of public anticipation approached that of the Second Coming. Tsai had planned to sell around $25 million worth of shares, but on February 15, 1966, the date of the unveiling of what was regarded as the great new bandwagon to a new land of assured wealth, a fantastic $270 million poured in as the public dashed to climb aboard. "We came out at just the right time," says Tsai. "The psychology was bullish, the stock market was doing great and the people were in the mood to buy something new." The Manhattan Fund's inauguration was the height of Tsai's near-deification, and it ironically coincided almost precisely with the all-time high of the Dow Jones Average.

Tsai set up Manhattan Fund just like Fidelity Capital. He loaded it with all of his big glamor favorites. To facilitate his chartist maneuverings, he built an elaborate trading room with a Trans-Jets tape, a Quotron electronic board with the prices of relevant securities and three-foot-square, giant loose-leaf notebooks filled with Point- and Figure-charts and other technical indicators for all his holdings. Adjoining the trading room was erected "Information Central," so aswarm with visual displays and panels that slid and rotated about that it resembled some Pentagon war room. Three men were hired to work full-time maintaining literally hundreds of averages, ratios, oscillators and indices, ranging from a "10-day oscillator of differences in advances and declines," to charts of several Treasury issues, to 25-, 65- and 150-day moving averages for the Dow. "We keep everything," says Walter Deemer, a former Merrill Lynch analyst and boss of Information Central who regards his charts the way an expert horticulturist might regard a bed of prize geraniums. "You may only want a certain graph once a year, but when you do, it's here."

Despite its auspicious beginnings, 1966 turned cloudy and threatening and by year-end the Dow slumped 20 per cent. Manhattan Fund did respectably, if not spectacularly, declining only 6 per cent. The market recovered in 1967 and again Tsai's stock zoomed upward. Manhattan Fund was up 40 per cent, well over double the Dow, and the best record of any fund its size. Tsai was still doing everything right. In the last quarter of 1967, he unloaded his vast airline holdings (including 300,000 shares of American) with such a great flourish that he was widely accused of "killing the airlines." (The airlines, of course, had killed themselves, and are selling way below their 1967 highs.)

Tsai's success is well illustrated by his "Super Glamor Average" in Information Central. The S.G.A. records the percentage of weekly changes in sixteen issues such as Avon, Burroughs, Fairchild Camera, Teledyne and Zenith. The graph begins at 10 in 1961 and then, with barely a pause even for the 1962 market break, it rises up and up to near 70 in December of 1967.

Tsai began 1968 with $500 million in a group of forty stocks which look like a typical Tsai portfolio for any time in the previous ten years: lots of data processing (Control Data, IBM); electronics (Collins Radio, General Instrument, Itek, Raytheon, Teledyne); office equipment (Burroughs, National Cash Register); along with touches of conglomerates (Gulf & Western, Walter Kidde, LTV); some oils, and his long-time loves, Polaroid and Sperry Rand.

At the time, Tsai did harbor some worries that perhaps the era of the big glamor stocks was coming to a close. In a speech in January to the First Annual Institutional Investor Conference, he stated that while "we see no reason to alter our basic approach to investment," he did see increasing interest in a "new generation" of growth stocks: "My own feeling is that we are now in the midst of a new investment cycle, marked by the same sort of birth pains that accompany most market downturns . . ." Tsai says today he had actually thought about calling his speech "The Big Switch" and much more flatly predicting that "growth stocks had had it."

"But I didn't do anything about it," he declares. "By the end of 1967, the glamor stocks were way ahead of themselves; they had become way overpriced. The charts kept telling us they were not the most desirable areas but we were too dumb to realize it." While other performance funds, no longer following Tsai's every move, eagerly switched to small, usually over-the-counter special situations such as mobile-home makers and franchisers, or at least took refuge in the Dow Jones Average-type stocks, Tsai (and a number of the other large growth fund managers) sat for months waiting for his glamor stocks to move. Instead, the lines on the "Super Glamor Average" beat a rocky retreat downward toward 50.

Given Tsai's predilection for hastily unloading what is not producing, his misjudgment may seem difficult to comprehend. Many of Tsai's detractors maintain that Tsai, in the words of one, ". . . was always a trader, never an investor, who thought his game was the only game in town," and that in a different market environment, he was like a fish caught out of water. While this may be somewhat unfair, it is true that while it was one thing for Tsai to trade aggressively in individual stocks, it was quite another thing for him to abandon an entire category of stocks that had been his trademark, that invariably, ever since he started managing other people's money, had been on the up side, outstripped the Dow and made him a winner. One must also realize how alien the hot new issues were to him, issues with tiny capitalizations that would not allow him to concentrate his portfolio and that did not possess the quality Tsai values so dearly: marketability. He kept remembering what happened to these stocks in 1962. "If the market goes down, you have to get out of them at sacrifice prices," he says. "Maybe you sell your first thousand shares a dollar and a half off but then you're told there just isn't a market any more." A retreat to the Dow stocks was also difficult: with the spotlight on Manhattan Fund's performance, suppose he had been tied up with a bunch of steel stocks when his glamors took off again?

Tsai, decidedly an up-market man, found himself trapped in the traditional down-market psychology. "Mr. Johnson used to tell me that investors—and the fund manager is just the same as the man in the street—always get fear and hope mixed up," he says. "When their stocks are going down they keep hoping they will recover when they should be fearful that they won't and sell." Only belatedly, therefore, did Tsai finally sell huge blocks of Collins Radio, Control Data, Burroughs and the rest. Some situations, including a huge 250,000 share holding of Gulf & Western, he continued to ride all the way down. As G&W sank over 50 per cent he kept maintaining that it "still seems like a terribly good buy."

There was, too, a serious organization problem. Tsai has a great desire to build organizations under himself, but he has difficulty in consolidating what he has built. He persists in running a kind of one-man show, and refuses to delegate sufficient authority to free himself from the press of minutiae. Thus while he was personally supervising every detail of the Manhattan Fund, from picking stocks to researching information to buying and selling blocks, he was also starting up a host of new projects: The Liberty Fund; the leveraged

TMR Appreciation Fund; Fundex; a dual-purpose, closed-end fund listed on the NYSE called the Hemisphere Fund; a venture capital operation; an investment counseling business—and, during 1968, negotiating the deal with CNA. At one point, he had tried to hand over management of the Manhattan Fund to Robert Campbell, Jr., who now runs TMR Appreciation, but Tsai spent so much time watching over Campbell's shoulder and second-guessing him that the arrangement was discontinued after a few months. As a result, says a former Tsai M&R executive, "Jerry just didn't spend enough time with Manhattan Fund. He missed most of the good groups last year because he was too busy doing other things."

Published reports of Manhattan Fund's sagging performance seriously compounded Tsai's troubles. As his geniushood was judged to have mysteriously slipped away, Manhattan Fund was flooded with requests from shareholders to buy back their shares. By the end of the year these redemptions were to mushroom to an incredible $181 million against only $41 million in purchases. "Publicity builds you and it can kill you," Tsai sighs. This development required much forced selling and a virtual destruction of Tsai's traditional strategy of adjusting the cash/securities ratio to take advantage of market fluctuations. "At one point we forecast, correctly as it turned out, a market drop, and we went from 95 per cent in cash to 84 per cent," he relates. "But the redemptions pushed us right back up to 95 per cent. By the end of 1968, Manhattan Fund's net assets had dropped from $560 million to $381 million. It is difficult to imagine the degree of personal anguish and embarrassment Tsai must have suffered.

Manhattan Fund during the first four months of 1969 declined another 4.4 per cent, but few of the other performance funds have done much better, and many of the small go-go funds did much worse. (It is interesting to note that the record during 1968 and early 1969 of Fidelity Capital and Fidelity Trend, also heavy in big glamor securities, has been almost as bad as Manhattan Fund.) Tsai's biggest position at year-end 1968, Northwest Industries, has also been his biggest loser. Stymied in its attempt to take over B. F. Goodrich, Northwest declined to half its high last December, from over $140 (pre-split) to the $70's. "At $100 a share, earning $8 it certainly wasn't high," Tsai maintains. "At $90 it seems cheaper, at $80 you just can't stand to sell. The question is: do you look at value or not? If you don't sell at $100, you should be buying at $80." Nevertheless, Tsai recently cut his position by two-thirds.

But Tsai still remains convinced that the glamor stocks' excesses of 1967 have been compensated for. "Though their prices were flat during 1968, the earnings have continued to go up, so their p/e ratios have been going down. I think they are once again ready to outperform the market." His favorites for fall 1969 and the 1970's are IBM, Avon, Burroughs and Sperry Rand. His reasoning on Sperry Rand is typical of the way he views these stocks and his portfolio choices in general: "Sperry's been selling in the 50's and we think it's going to earn $2.50. If the market doesn't fumble and if nothing hurts the computer stocks, Sperry's p/e could go from 20 to 25, since historically the company's p/e has always gone up when it's earnings did. If Sperry makes $2.50 and it seems on the way to $3, then the p/e could go even higher, maybe 30. So, maybe we're talking about a $90 stock."

The complexion of Manhattan Fund is now changing since Tsai hired two portfolio managers and at last resolved to let others take over the day-to-day management. The men are moving the fund into smaller companies that Tsai never would have looked at, such as the gambling stocks, and companies active in mortgage investment, real estate and nursing homes. Tsai has permitted this radical shift with some reluctance. When one of the new men rushed in not long ago to tell Tsai, "We've got to get into some of these land companies," Tsai finally agreed, but ruled that the holdings be limited to 2 per cent of the portfolio. "It was a little like me trying to sell Xerox and Polaroid to Mr. Johnson ten years ago," he says.

Tsai's big interest now is his new career as a corporate builder. "If I were not in this business," he says, "I would have liked to be an architect." The Manhattan Fund logo, the skyline of a city, an illuminated three-dimensional plastic version of which adorns his office, is Tsai's own design. His two weekend homes in Connecticut are full of his own ideas. The first, which he sold, was in Weston; the current one is in Greenwich. In both cases, older, more conventional houses at first occupied the property. Both were immediately razed and replaced with low, sleek, glass and fieldstone structures. The Greenwich plot is right on the Sound, and Tsai tells enthusiastically how he designed and had erected on the beach a 400-foot sea wall, which along with some sixty-eight tons of dirt, "created three acres of lawn out of no place."

In interviews Tsai has stated that the chief reason for selling Tsai M&R to CNA was that he "needed the established sales network" for his funds. But the key provision of the deal was that Tsai was made executive vice-president of CNA, with responsibility for developing non-insurance mergers and acquistions, which CNA is actively seeking.

Some of Tsai's friends feel that he never would have sold to CNA and given up his independence unless he had received assurances that he at least had a good shot at the presidency—Howard C. Reeder, sixty-three, is both president and chairman.

Says Tsai, who is CNA's biggest stockholder, about his job: "It's not just picking a company and seeing the stock go up. You have to convince the seller to sell, you have to convince the CNA management and the directors, you have to bargain, work out the terms, negotiate with the lawyers . . . it's much more challenging." He personally arranged two of CNA's most important recent acquisitions, Kane Financial Corp., which is involved in nursing homes and land development, and the Larwin Group of Companies, the country's largest privately owned home builders. (He brought off the latter deal, which is yet to be voted on, despite the fact that Larwin was romanced by dozens of other companies and batallions of investment bankers who wanted to make them public.)

"They are all building blocks," he continues. "One thing leads to another. Already we have insurance, mutual funds, personal loans, home building. What's next? Hotels? We're already doing that. We're building a big hotel in Hawaii. Travel agencies? Title search? Leasing companies? Mortgage finance companies? We're putting a consumer service company together with a finance company. Some day we may have hundreds of CNA financial centers all over the country like Howard Johnsons where people can walk in off the street and buy insurance, do their banking, borrow money, plan vacations, get their income tax done. The insurance company is the money machine. It grinds out the cash flow. It's kind of an inverse triangle."

He holds his hands close together on the table, then slowly raises them and spreads them far, far apart. He looks at his hands for a moment, then adds with a very scrutable smile, "Of course, this is just my dream."

MISTER JOHNSON
Where performance was born:
equal portions of Eric Hoffer
Maria Montessori & Buddha

LTHOUGH JERRY TSAI was its first important practitioner, the origin of performance as an investment concept traces back a little more than a quarter of a century ago, to the time when a quiet Boston lawyer named Edward C. Johnson II acquired a small firm called Fidelity Management and Research and began to mold it into a rather special place where money was managed in a way it had never been managed before. "Mister Johnson," as this dean of money managers is almost universally described, accomplished the revolution by creating an environment—unique then and unusual even now—where individuals could devise their own individual strategies toward the overall goal of achieving maximum gains.

The results of this experiment were great. Most significantly, Fidelity showed everyone that aggressive, intensive money management with emphasis on capital appreciation could produce consistent, superior gains without undue risk, and that satisfaction with a fixed, annual yield on one's investment was unrealistic and imprudent. Fidelity also produced a wide variety of other practices which have today become synonomous with investment professionalism: notably the use of charts and the courting of Wall Street analysts by acting on their information and paying for it rapidly with commission business. The key to its success was its avowed cultivation of the individual, which attracted and developed such legendary masters as Jerry Tsai and Roland Grimm, whose careers are described elsewhere in these pages. Above all, Fidelity seems to have acquired a quality larger than its success in investing other people's money. Old Fidelians, even those who no longer work there, speak of it with the lavish nostalgia usually reserved for places like Scott Fitzgerald's Princeton. They may have moved on (sigh) but that was where it all came alive.

If you ask what this enthusiasm rests upon, they invariably mention "freedom" and "individualism." But it is not simply that the funds under management are left to individual portfolio managers rather than a committee. Fidelity's freedom is something more extreme and more pervasive.

It all comes back, everyone agrees, to the man who took over the place twenty-six years ago. "Fidelity," says one Street chartist, "is the lengthened shadow of Mr. Johnson."

Mr. Johnson is spare, sprightly, and though he is seventy-one he possesses enormous but restrained energy and a boyish delight in ideas. One associate describes him as a "mild-mannered, Clark Kent type of guy." Typically his conversation turns to fairly cosmic ideas, and he seems very much at home with them. When he talks he holds his hands out, as if catching a volley ball or measuring a fish. What he is doing is shaping concepts.

Mr. Johnson does not like to be pinned down. If you ask him how he runs the institution, for instance, he scurries away. "Oh, I don't run anything. It runs itself," he says. "I'm just an assistant." He describes Fidelity's recent activities as something with which he has only a tenuous connection. "The diversification of the management company is something I watch with fascination," he will say. When asked when he will retire from doing whatever it is he does there, he tosses the question away as if it were rather rude. "I have no idea when," he replies, then follows with a devastating piece of self-effacement. "The ideal is that when you appear in the death columns people will say, 'Oh, isn't he here any more?'"

This is not all false modesty. When you ask his employees what kind of influence he exerts, they describe it in the same way. "He has run the company by not showing himself, sort of like Buddha," says one Fidelity man. Perhaps Mr. Johnson, an ardent student of Eastern philosophy, thinks of himself a little that way too: ruling by what one of his favorite writers, Zen expert Alan W. Watts, calls "the law of reversed effort," whereby "nothing is more powerful and creative than emptiness."

Certainly he tries to leave those around him as empty as possible. The one who compares him to Buddha notes that "Mr. Johnson has instant recall on the stock market. He can tell you what the market did on June 2, 1936. Yet he never exerts pressure on you. He never says: 'This is what happened ten years ago so now I think you should do this.' You have to go to him and ask him what he thinks of the current situation. Even then he may throw the question back at you."

From this, a picture of what freedom means at Fidelity begins to emerge. Mr. Johnson describes its purpose this way: "You want an environment where people can develop their talents to the greatest extent. How do you do that? It's just one word: attitude. You want the greatest degree of *laissez faire* without chaos. Children know you love them and that you're always there and otherwise you leave them alone and that's it. That's the way it is here, too, I think. What you want to get away from is an organization and create an organism. Separate cells working together in something completely natural and unplanned."

What is the raw material for this process? What kind of man excells in such an environment? Here, again, Mr. Johnson is so nebulous that the answers almost seem not to be answers. "We want a man with an instinctive sense of value, an artist," he says. "Investing is like any art. We don't want the theoretical man with a lot of words, the so-called intellectual. We like the young man who will come in and not have ideas that are too firm and counter to our own. This doesn't mean we don't want a high level of difference of opinion; we thrive on it. I love prima donnas. They blow off steam and then go off and do something artistic again."

With so little direction, how do you recognize the good people?

"The cruel end result is in the funds. With stocks, in the long run you will see."

How do you hold the people who survive this test?

You don't. "We start off with the assumption that when you get somebody good and he pays off in a big way it's difficult to hold him. When he goes off, believe it or not, this is a strengthening thing. Besides, a star is at his best on the way up. Somebody leaving to go after a glamorous future is the best possible incentive for the men here."

There is one element missing from Mr. Johnson's picture of the Fidelity environment, and that is the mechanism that creates this organism of individualistic artistic prima donnas. Is it just the warm happy bath of freedom in which they are swimming? Hardly, to hear Mr. Johnson speak. For when he talks about the process that develops people, he says things like "struggle and trouble bring out the most glorious flavors." Or "change is what matters. If you read Eric Hoffer the way I do, you realize that change is a painful and often soul-wrenching experience."

Let's begin at the beginning, the recruiting process, to see how Fidelity goes about creating performers. Recently, though Fidelity has no set criteria for its employees, a lot of the new analysts have come from Harvard Business School. Executive vice-president George Sullivan, who does most of the hiring, says that he interviews thirty-five to forty B-School men each year just about summer jobs.

Yet Fidelity, though the school is a mere ten minutes up the river, never follows the usual practice of installing an interviewer there for a day and running people quickly by him.

"Fidelity doesn't reach out and grab you; you have to fight your way in," says one recent recruit, Richard C. Habermann. "It's a correspondence operation. They just put this little notice up on the board that says, 'If you're interested, write and tell us why.' When you go for interviews they practically lean back in a chair, fold their arms, and say 'Well?' You have to make the effort to prove in that short time that you could be useful to them."

Actually, interviews last quite a long time compared to

those at many investment houses. "When I came I think I saw five people for one-and-a-half to two hours each," Habermann continues. "This was a marked contrast to the regimented system at some investment banking houses in New York. You'd have a half-hour appointment with some guy and he'd get a phone call in the middle of it and talk for fifteen minutes, and then you had fifteen minutes in all because he had somebody booked right after you.

"This place, on the other hand, really gave you the feeling that they wanted to get to know you. The guy might be on the phone for the first half hour of your interview, but he'd still see you for a couple of hours after that."

So even the recruiting process at Fidelity might be called "artistic," with "an instinctive sense of value" rather than a check list. This is partly because Fidelity is looking for rather indefinable characteristics. "I don't care what a fellow's background is," says FMR's president George Sullivan, who interviews about two hundred and fifty people a year. "What I'm interested in is curiosity, a desire to learn, and fascination with this business."

What all this adds up to is a picture like the one sketched vaguely by Mr. Johnson. The interviewer's instincts are much more important than a check list. From the start, the candidate is drawn out rather than bored into. He has to find his own path to travel. There are no road signs.

The training process is similarly formless. If you ask people at Fidelity to describe it, their initial reaction is to break into a broad grin. Training in the sense of being told how to examine a report or a company, or being told what criteria to use to establish whether a stock is a buy or sell—training even in the simplest sense of being told what or whom to ask—simply doesn't exist. Habermann, for instance, who came to Fidelity with no industry experience, places the period during which somebody held his hand at about two weeks.

And the hand wasn't very firmly held even then. Habermann started at Fidelity as an oil analyst, taking over from Richard M. Smith who became one of the portfolio managers of Fidelity's Trend Fund. "He gave me all this garbage to read and said, 'Go learn about the oil industry for two weeks.' Then I was off on my first trip. Alone. After I saw about five companies, I wrote reports with recommendations. Dick Smith's comments? He said 'huh' and sent them on to the investment committee. Unedited, they ended up being the basis of investment decisions."

This obviously says something about the quality of those reports, but it also says a lot about the Fidelity modus operandi. In this case, at least, Habermann said it had very good effects. Because no one told him how to judge a company, he developed a different set of standards from those that were in vogue at the time. "As a result, we took a big position that's been very successful," he says.

How, then, does one learn at Fidelity? Where do the impulses come from?

Here comes that nebulousness again. "All this thing is pure contagion," says Mr. Johnson. "The great golfers were caddies who watched the good players." George Sullivan speaks of training rookies by "immersing them in a team of experienced people." Another Fidelity executive describes it more like a cockfight. "You get people with strong opinions," he says, "toss them into the pot and let them argue it out."

Either way, the principle is one of simple exposure to others. If you give the right man such exposure, Mr. Johnson believes, the result can be exciting. "I have a theory," he says, "that if a person has talent that's oriented in the general direction of the stock market, he and the market together will develop a personality beyond anything else he could have developed alone. So many things affect his work that finding out about them gives him a voraciousness for life. The free exchange of ideas, the intellectual equivalent of rubbing elbows, develops his talent to the greatest extent."

Thus, it is quite strange that Fidelity, where training is so pointedly unspecific, unregimented, and indescribable in specific terms, should have a reputation as the great trainer of people in the investment business. Fidelity has often been described as a university, but it is surely a university in which all classes are seminars rather than lectures, and in which all the participants both teach and learn. It all sounds rather like a Montessori kindergarten.

It is not just during the recruiting and training process that a man is made to feel alone and on his own, of course. The process carries over into Fidelity's everyday existence. Up to now—and this may change as Fidelity continues to grow in size—a deliberate effort has been made to play down structure and hierarchy. To be sure, there is an investment committee, there are people with titles who are above other people. But in investment, as opposed to administration, distinctions among people are played down as much as possible. In Fidelity's management booklet, which introduces Fidelity's key sixty or so employees, fund managers who are not officers of the management company itself are grouped with the analysts under the heading "research" and they are described not as managers of this or that fund but rather as having "special portfolio assignments."

One reason for leaving the designations in the booklet vague is that they change often. Analysts at Fidelity cannot expect to settle down with an industry comfortably for the rest of their lives. In general, Fidelity encourages its people to look for new assignments, and moves them around as much as possible.

Just as there is little structure in the company—an organization chart is unthinkable—there is little structure in the communications system. System? A fund manager may rely on in-house research people, or he may rely on people in the Street or at companies. He may or may not communicate with his own analysts, and the communication may proceed from the analyst to the fund manager or vice versa.

Does the extreme formlessness of the Fidelity environment get people to work by making them anxious?

"The freedom here does create anxiety," says Roger L. Clinton, whose fund has been doing poorly recently. "And I think this is exactly the intent. It's cruel and frustrating at times. It's very much like Darwinism. There are some people who might be more efficient if they had more guidance, but they have to develop in a different way to survive here. All of us might be happier, but the question is what is most important? Mr. Johnson thinks it's the development of the individual. He thinks that every little bit of structure you add takes something away from the human being."

One element of the anxiety is simple competitiveness. Since the fund prospectuses are vague—designed specifically to allow the fund to take on the personality of its manager— several have essentially identical objectives. "The result," says Allen W. B. Gray, a four-year Fidelity veteran, "is that you are competing not just with other funds outside Fidelity but inside too." The Trend Fund has three separate sections managed by three different people, and the competition among the three is intense.

"It's a risky environment," Gray sums up, "but—that's life I guess." Thus, Fidelity consciously creates an environment in which only those who can bear the strain of being completely undirected will survive. It is an organization of loners: people who must decide what paths to walk down on their own. And the business of finding one's own path is the business of doing something new. Fidelity's ability as an innovator proceeds directly from this loner environment.

"I think one of Mr. Johnson's great credos," says FMR's executive vice-president William L. Byrnes, "is that we don't know how it's going to turn out. This is a cut and fit operation. It's a willingness to experiment. If someone came and said 'we've got to have a bond fund' I don't think Mr. Johnson would say no automatically."

In the past, innovations have sprung from this spirit, so it is interesting to see what Fidelity is up to today. The direction in which the firm is heading is best illustrated by the purchase, in mid-1967, of the Equity Fund, a $40 million fund operated separately from Seattle. At first glance the acquisition would seem unusual, since the fund is small, little-known and sold in only four Midwestern states. But in the context of what Fidelity plans, the move makes sense; it is a small, satellite operation, separately managed but still within the firm's money management specialty. Other fields in which Fidelity is beginning to get its feet wet: venture capital, an off-shore fund and a system to run money by computer.

A major role in shaping Fidelity's future will be played by Edward C. Johnson III, Mr. Johnson's son, who recently was promoted to executive vice-president of the firm and quite clearly is the heir apparent.

On the surface, Ned Johnson may seem to be just one more

homogeneous link in a chain that stretches back to the Boston of 1635. When Ned Johnson married the former Elizabeth B. Hodges, in Nahant, in 1960, one of the pews in the church bore a small brass plaque reading "Edward C. Johnson," indicating that Ned's great-great uncle—Edward C. Johnson I—had spent his summers in this Boston suburb, which was at that time, the mid-nineteenth century, a small resort inhabited mostly by Boston Brahmins (not necessarily the city's most chic residents, but those whose lineage put them firmly in its aristocracy).

Ned Johnson spent his childhood in Milton, Mass., summering in the house his family moved to in 1937 at Cataumet on Cape Cod, where he swam, sailed, and played tennis. His big loves in school and college were athletics and photography. He traveled through a succession of Boston-area schools before ending up at his father's alma mater, Harvard, where he majored in Social Relations.

After serving in the Army, he spent the ritual year in a bank, deciding what he wanted to do. "I guess every son of every father goes through this period," he says. He took aptitude tests at the time which suggested he become a senior CPA or a musician. Odd choices, he thinks, as "I can't stand the tedium of accounting and I have a tin ear." He did want to do something "artistic," however, if not musical, and so went to Fidelity, whose founder continually refers to the fund manager as an artist.

Today, Ned Johnson and his family live in a house on Charles River Square, a graceful street of old townhouses, which lies on one boundary of the heart of the old city. It is furnished throughout with early American antiques, his major hobby. Johnson knows the fluting on an eighteenth-century highboy as well as the earnings record of IBM. He may greet a visitor in his slightly sterile sitting-room, where he sits uncomfortably on a formal settee, on whose silken upholstery a small speckled cat is exercising its claws. Oriental rugs lap over each other on the floor. Portraits of two maternal ancestors, as yet unhung, face him across the room from their perch atop two hi-fi speakers that flank a Townsend Gardiner highboy.

When they're not at their Montessori school, his three children break the museum house's stillness. It is a distinctive twist on the Old Fidelity legend of not directing individuals that their paternal grandfather thinks the children's upbringing is on the permissive side.

Indeed Ned Johnson has a number of ideas different from his father's. For one thing, he is more of a force for diversification than his father. "Our future expansion will be done through new operations," he explains. "The basic business will grow, but because of its size it can't grow as fast in percentage terms. Also, I think a research operation doesn't function well beyond a certain size. We want to remain a group of small, fighting teams. Ten years from now the body will be no larger but it will have more appendages."

Ned's biggest problem, though, is very current. During the past year, Fidelity's two big growth funds, Growth and Capital, have performed extremely poorly, worse in fact than the vast majority of other mutual funds. One problem may be that the Fidelity funds have simply become too large to rack up their former impressive percentage gains.

Reaction to the bad performance seems surprisingly calm, at least on the higher levels. And the justifications have almost a shoulder-shrugging air to them. "Rightly or wrongly," says Ned Johnson, "we took the viewpoint that we didn't want to get into these very small situations, the situations, for instance, which took some funds to the top in 1967 and 1968." The spectre of 1962 was what kept the Fidelity funds in fairly solid, big-time stuff the last two years.

Mr. Johnson seems less concerned than his son. He notes a little sheepishly that "any organization, in its growth, comes to a point where it consolidates." Of the future he says, "Oh heavens, you don't care about that. I guess my viewpoint is very strong on the future: I ignore it. It's so silly. You can't love the future. You can't eat it. You can't drink it. By thinking about the future you take all the vitality out of it. Aim to do whatever you're doing better and let the future take care of itself."

Still, there is a lot of rustling in the Fidelity underbrush, and a lot of changes are being made—very fundamental changes in both research and portfolio management. In the research area, Fidelity is reexamining the whole fabric of relationships among its account managers, in-house analysts, the brokers they deal with, and the companies they do research on.

Most of the changes focus on upgrading the role of the analyst. This in itself is a departure for Fidelity. There has been little structure at Fidelity, but one thing was sure: the account managers were the elite. "The Jerry Tsai syndrome," explains one ten-year Fidelian, "has had a great effect on how a portfolio manager is regarded here. So you can make everything else equal—pay and so forth—and still have an analyst feel that the only way he can make it big is to run some money."

In order to increase the visibility and effectiveness of the analyst, Fidelity plans to introduce more order into its communications system, and to monitor more closely the performance of its analysts.

A major thrust will be to educate the analyst on how to get the account manager's attention. "I want him to learn how to put the account manager in the position where he has to take the guy's research into account—whether he chooses to act on it or not," says research coordinator John Ames. It is perhaps a surprise that this sort of education is necessary. "But it is," he contends. "I think there's a tendency to assume that because the analysts are all dolled up with M.B.A.'s and such—they know how to use their time."

One way an analyst can attract notice is to use the competition between managers to force a decision. "When I used to return from a trip all enthusiastic I'd rip down the hall and try to sell somebody on it," Ames says. "I might have gone to Tsai for instance and found that he couldn't see me, so then I'd talk to Ned and if I sold him on it I'd go back and leave Jerry a little note. 'Dear Jerry,' it would say, 'I have seen company A and I think it's a great idea for Capital.— John. P.S. I have already talked to Ned and he is buying it for Trend.' This worked amazingly well."

If it's impossible to get to a manager or to convince him on your story, Ames recommends that the analyst write a report directly to the investment committee. There is a lot of antagonism built into this system, as you can see.

It is not just the relationships among the various people involved in its research work that Fidelity is overhauling; the way in which the company does research also seems to be headed for a significant change.

One possibility is that Fidelity will establish a sort of in-house think tank. Says George Sullivan, "We may hire several people who are just paid to think." The first has already been hired. A former conglomerate analyst, he will, presumably, consider such questions as: If LTV has a steel company, will everyone want them? If so, maybe we should buy steel companies across the board.

Another possible change is that while analysts have tended to work alone, as the research staff grows analysts may work into groups and study stocks in groups. The groups will probably not be divided into industries but into more imaginative divisions such as glamor stocks, money rate stocks, low p/e stocks, mass communications and so forth. And because of recent controversy over what constitutes inside information, Fidelity is going to place increasing emphasis on talking to a company's competitors and suppliers, and less on talking to its officers.

But not all Fidelity's changes at its Boston headquarters center on research. Recently, Fidelity has changed how it manages its two biggest funds, Trend and Capital.

The first change is to split them among separate portfolio managers, and is not unique to Fidelity. A similar system has been tried at Enterprise and, in a different form, at the Competitive Capital Fund.

Ultimately Fidelity may assign Trend, now under two men, to four managers. Though competition can be expected to be strong, Ned Johnson believes new money coming into the fund will not be allocated according to performance, "though we might divide new flows unevenly on the basis of whether we're in the kind of a market we think is a guy's specialty, or according to the optimum size of money he seems able to manage well."

More unusual is the system being tried in Capital Fund. Starting in January 1969, two men began to comanage it, which is a radically new approach to managing bigness. The system is not competitive for the men will not split the fund up and manage their pieces separately unless they find they disagree consistently. Nor does it combine manager and an assistant manager, a system Fidelity uses with some funds but which it may chuck because several assistant managers have felt it to be an unproductive use of their time.

Still, it is not quite a committee approach, either. For one thing, two is too small a crowd. More importantly, they expect to mesh two different approaches on how to invest big money, not simply decide together which particular stocks to buy and sell.

The future of Fidelity, of course, depends more than anything else on Ned Johnson, and more than others in the firm, he stresses the need for modifying the policy of nondirection. "We sometimes haven't told people when they do something wrong two or three times," he says, "and we haven't always praised them when they've done well, either. I think we may have carried our ideas too far, which could be a subconscious reason people have left. From now on, if someone's off course we're going to start sooner to steer him back."

This change is just a part of what Ned Johnson seems to talk about most: the need to gear up in order to be able to diversify. "The way the company is growing," he says, "we have to set up measures and controls for many different businesses. It's a matter of being able to look at a limited number of statistics and talk briefly to a few people to know what's going on in your company. If something goes wrong, you get in there fast and operate. You also want to be able to put out fires fast enough so that you don't use up all the creativity of your people who are running the company.

"Quite frankly," he goes on, "setting up these controls is our main job over the next two or three years. When this is done, we can have an awful lot of fun."

A. W. JONES
Hedge funds:
the long and the short way
to beat the market

WHILE MANY of the money management pioneers have faded into obscurity or comfortable old age, a decided exception is a sixty-eight-year-old man named A. W. Jones. Many others have picked up his ideas, but none has yet been able to match his success.

The firm of A. W. Jones and Co., was founded just twenty years ago by Alfred Winslow Jones, a transplanted journalist and sociologist who was the first to operate consistently on the *hedging* principle. Once others penetrated the secret of how he was operating, there was a massive outpouring of imitators. There are now well over a hundred hedge funds managing several billions of dollars, and they have become the ultimate in today's market—the logical extension of the current gunslinging, go-go cult of success. They rack up far and away the biggest gains, year after year; they get into and out of stock faster, and they generate more in commissions for brokers than just about any other type of investment. Even so, by all accounts his fund is still the biggest and best performing of this proliferating body of hedge funds. Over the last decade, A. W. Jones and Co. has made a gain of well over 1,000 per cent on its assets, and the fund now manages something on the order of $200 million.

Depending on whom you talk to, hedge fund managers are either magicians who have found a way to make money without worrying about market setbacks, or else bearish ogres who gamble wildly on margin. Yet, A. W. Jones spelled out the standards for hedge funds rather clearly, and the pattern he set has endured. In brief here is what hedge funds are:

—They are private pools of capital that bring together groups of wealthy individuals who each generally contribute $100,000, $250,000 or even more.

—They leverage these assets to the hilt, multiplying their effectiveness by buying some securities on margin and borrowing on others.

—They attract some of the top investment talent to run their money because they offer extraordinarily high rewards; their managers get a piece of the action: up to 20 per cent of the fund's profits.

—They are formed legally as private partnerships, meaning that by existing rules of the game they are not subject to the jurisdiction of the Securities and Exchange Commission.

The hedge comes in when the funds sell short, and the way Jones figured it there were very real reasons why this should be done all the time. By consistently selling a portion of his portfolio short he could offer a dollop of extra protection to his investors. "The logic of the idea was very clear," he says. "It was a hedge against the vagaries of the market. You could

buy more good stocks without taking as much risk as someone who merely bought."

A. W. Jones has an easy smile and white hair that is a bit
thin in the front; he really isn't cut from any mold that might
be considered remotely typical of Wall Street. He is still very
much the head of A. W. Jones and Co.—though most of the
day-to-day decision-making in securities has been turned
over to a team of bright young money managers; but he is
also a working sociologist whose chief attention at the
moment is directed to solving the problems of poverty.

In the era of the star system, with each successive go-go
performer being thrust into the public spotlight, he has generally shunned publicity. He prefers the reflective world of
concepts and ideas, and has rarely been interviewed. In dress,
his orthodox pinstripe suits may be rounded off with brightly
colored ties and pocket handkerchiefs and sporty buckled
loafers in the modern style.

However, the unique aspect about Alfred Jones—and a
good many of the investors who have profited by becoming
partners in his operation—is what the money itself means to
them. Jones frankly says that he wanted to make money in
Wall Street because he eventually hoped to be able "to slope
away from business and pick up my old interest in social
affairs." Moreover, he wanted his limited partners, many of
whom were active in scientific and artistic fields, to be free
from financial worries so that they could devote themselves
entirely to creative efforts.

It was a lofty—if somewhat unusual—approach to Wall
Street, the kind of thing many dream about but few accomplish. Jones puts it this way: "Too many men don't want to
do something *after* they make money. They just go on and
make a lot more money."

Jones readily admits that his firm probably could have made a great deal more money by being "way out long" rather than hedged. But he considers that "an imprudent policy. It would have been improper to do so because we are handling other people's money." Hedging by selling a portion of the portfolio short, he contends, is basically using a speculative tool for conservative purposes, and without it, he says, "I would not have been able to sleep so well at night."

The term selling short, incidentally, has backed into the language in rather a curious way. It is used, of course, to express sentiments like, "Don't sell my secretary short—she may not wear a mini-skirt, but she takes shorthand at 200 words a minute." But it has a very specific market meaning. You've seen the new Acme Motors models, let's say, and you don't think they will sell and you think the stock will drop. So your broker scouts around for someone who will lend you a hundred shares and he sells them for cash. All you have to do is return those shares some time in the future. And since you think the price of Acme is going down, you hope to buy the shares back later for less money, leaving you with a profit. It is a bit more complicated than that, since you have to put up margin with your broker when you borrow, but that is the gist of the idea.

Alfred Jones discusses such business matters articulately, of course, speaking in a soft voice. But when the conversation turns to social affairs, he becomes eloquent. His basic concern is with what he calls "the humiliated poor"; he considers their poverty "a national disgrace." He has set up a foundation which is working with the U.S. Bureau of Social Services to investigate the causes of social disruptions. He currently is directing a team of researchers working on specific programs to solve poverty problems. While Jones concludes that industry can do a great deal more to help, he believes that it will take "a generation before most of the unemployables can be promoted into the mainstream of American life."

A. W. Jones was born in Australia, the son of a General Electric executive who was posted there around the turn of the century. His family soon returned to GE headquarters in Schenectady, where he grew up. Jones graduated from Harvard in 1923 and subsequently picked up a Ph.D. in sociology from Columbia. His doctoral thesis, which evolved from research he did on attitudes toward corporate property, was published under the title *Life, Liberty and Property*, and recently went into its third printing. Jones served for a time with the Foreign Service in Berlin during the 1930's, and after the book was published, *Fortune* hired him to condense it into an article. He went on to become an editor for Time-Life during the early 1940's, writing on a wide variety of subjects, ranging from business to boys' prep schools.

It was about this time that Jones got the idea he could make money in Wall Street. He undertook a free-lance assignment for *Fortune* concerning technical approaches to the market. The article, published in 1949, was entitled "Fashions in Forecasting." Jones saw this assignment as a means of meeting the people he wanted to know on the Street. "I would repudiate much of what I said in the article now," he says, "but it enabled me to make contacts." A. W. Jones and Co. was founded in 1949, with capital of only $100,000— $40,000 from Jones himself and the rest from four friends.

For more than a decade, the Jones operation was pretty much a closed affair. The manager of a now-successful hedge fund, who formerly worked for a brokerage house, explains why. "We could only see the top of the iceberg," he says. "We knew that Jones was making a fortune and that people who were associated with him were doing extremely well. But we didn't know how he was doing it."

The principles behind his operation began to leak out in the early and middle 1960's, and they set off shock waves. Jones, the stories went, might be short as many as sixty different stocks at any given time. Jones was using leverage like Archimedes. Jones was getting 20 per cent off the top when he was right. And Jones was right. The firm's record far outpaced that of any publicly owned mutual fund. Moreover, in 1962, when the market and other funds slumped badly, Jones actually showed a small gain.

To show what Jones was doing, let's example how a hypothetical hedge fund with $10 million in assets works. First we will assume the fund is leveraged 40 per cent; that is, it has bought some listed securities at 80 per cent margin and has borrowed money from a bank on some of its over-the-counter securities. This means that the fund's money is working at 140 per cent effectiveness. However, if the market trend, though on the upside, shows signs of weakness, the fund might keep 110 per cent of its leveraged portfolio on the long side, and 30 per cent in securities sold short. By hedge fund math, the "risk" or "exposure" position of this portfolio is the difference between those two figures: 80 per cent. A solid proportion of its long position thus is hedged against possible mistakes in realizing the market outlook.

In practice, of course, hedge fund managers hope to buy stocks which will rise more than average during up markets; indeed, they are able to be more aggressive on the long side *because* they have the hedge as a cushion. On the other hand, they try to select stocks for shorting that will perform worse than average in rising markets—or actually fall. As market conditions change, they can juggle their position, even going net short when general market declines appear to be in the offing.

This is where hedge funds have the advantage over mutual funds. In falling markets, the only course for most fund managers is to become defensive, increase their cash positions, and head for the sidelines. And if they keep a very high cash balance for a long time, they are in danger, as one hedge fund manager puts it, of being "redempted out"—of having a flood of investors redeem their shares, pulling their capital out of the fund.

But let's go back to our hypothetical $10 million portfolio. If the hedge fund can make 50 per cent during the course of a year—a not-unlikely possibility judging by past record—the fund manager's 20 per cent of the take amounts to $1 million. That is taxed at capital gains rates, too, since most hedge funds with their high-tax-bracket partners, are run for longer term gains. Thus the manager of our relatively small hedge fund can make, after taxes, a neat $750,000. As for the partners in the fund, they really don't mind paying him 20 per cent for his efforts because, after all, they have made a substantial gain on their own money. (With all that going for them, most hedge fund managers are reluctant to talk about their success. First of all, the big money follows success, and hedge fund managers already appear to be getting all the business they can handle. And second, they are wary of attracting further attention in Washington—the SEC is already conducting a detailed investigation of the impact of the hedge fund phenomenon—which might rock the boat.)

From the beginning, A. W. Jones and Co. was a rather unusual blend of the arts and the art of making money. The early investors in A. W. Jones, in addition to some businessmen, included writers, teachers, scholars, social workers and medical researchers. One of his first partners was Winslow Carlton, a long-time friend who is deeply involved in social welfare. Jones and his wife, Mary Carter, met Carlton while helping to raise funds for a Quaker civilian relief program during the Spanish Civil War. Another was Louis Fischer, prize-winning biographer (*The Life of Lenin*). A third investor who profited greatly from the success of the Jones organization was a woman who long headed one of the nation's most respected settlement houses. "She had a little stashed away," Jones recalls, "and now she is quite secure."

Jones calls such fallout "a gratifying aspect" of his firm's operations. "The people I knew who came along at the beginning have done well. In fact, they often tell me they are doing so well here that they can afford to devote themselves entirely to their most gratifying work."

A competitor who has known him for years says that "Alfred probably would have been considered a financial hippie in the 1950's. But he had a very simple little idea, and with the lure of 20 per cent of the profits was able to attract aggressive, capable young men into the organization. That's how the whole thing blossomed."

Jones' staffers stress the fact that there is no magic formula for making money with a fund operated on the hedged principle. Perhaps more than most kinds of investment management it depends on the brainpower of the man who runs the show.

A money manager, Jones says, must have "an interesting set of abilities." He needs vitality, aggressiveness and good judgment, of course. But beyond that, Jones stresses the fact that he must have two sets of balances. One is "a balance between boldness and caution." The other is a blend of "gullibility and skepticism." This, Jones explains, is because "a money manager doesn't dream up ideas. He gathers ideas from other sources. I've seen both extremes and the ultra-gullible is the worst because he can be led up the garden path. But being too skeptical is not very good either."

Successful money managers must also be tuned into the latest fads. "He must know what is coming into vogue, into fashion," Jones says, "because that is what he wants to have."

Today, the top echelon of hedge funds is dominated by partnerships that were launched by former Jones managers. Included are City Associates, which Carlisle Jones (no kin) started with Dean Milosis; Fairfield Partners of Greenwich, Conn., run by ex-Jones-partner Richard Radcliffee and Bart Briggs; and Cerberus Associates, managed by Ronald La-Bow. These funds, which have also shown remarkable performance records over the few years they have been in existence, each have in the area of $50 million or so in assets. Another Jones alumnus is investment counselor John Hartwell (p. 165).

Many nonalumni hedge managers got their inspiration to start hedge funds while working at houses that handled brokerage for the Jones hedge funds. In this roughly defined $20 million to $40 million category would be such partnerships as Fleschner-Becker Associates; Steinhardt, Fine & Berkowitz; Whitehall; Hanover Square; and Hawthorn Partners.

Yet even if they spring from the same philosophical concept, it is difficult to speak about hedge funds in broad terms. The Jones organization itself may have nearly as many different approaches to the market as it has fund managers (they number nearly ten). Each of the Jones portfolio managers brings his own experience and personality to bear on decision-making.

Jones and the men who work for him tend to shy away

from talking about specific stocks and specific figures. This general aloofness was underscored not long ago when the managers of another hedge fund, who have done extremely well in applying many of the Jones principles, decided to show their gratitude by inviting Mr. Jones to lunch. He demurred, and sent instead one of his associates who "handles that sort of thing."

Moreover, since fund managers are rapid traders, it is hard to speak of specific stocks which any particular Jonesman will like for more than a few weeks—or days, or even hours, for that matter. Indeed, the haste with which they can change opinions—and directions—sometimes seems arbitrary. A possibly apocryphal story tells of a Jones manager who took a huge position in Syntex before leaving for lunch not long ago. Whether something he ate disagreed with him, no one will ever know. But when he returned, he sold out the whole massive block.

The biggest problem facing hedge funds is the constant pressure to find good shorts, principally because the host of imitators Jones has spawned has narrowed down the opportunities. Picking shorts is a subtle art. Basically, it involves turning on their ear all the things one usually looks for in a stock—which can be a real wrench for traditionalists. Short hunters are after slow growth rates, not fast ones. They seek companies with weak management, not strong; and firms that are lagging badly in research and development. To take one case, not long ago everyone was making money in National Video, the so-called "IBM of the Shorts," a high-flier which was battered when strong competitors moved in on its color-TV tube market. National Video's chart looked like IBM's turned upside down.

A. W. Jones originally devised a complicated set of mathematical calculations for the "velocity" of individual stocks to help calculate how risky his investment position was at any given time. But today that approach has been de-emphasized. "Stocks don't act mathematically in the market," says Lester Kissel, managing partner of A. W. Jones and Co., who admits that the firm—like other hedge funds—no longer follows such calculations as "slavishly." Kissel stresses that "the calculation of the future based upon the past involves a certain amount of judgment, experience and 'feel.'"

While Jones himself no longer goes to his firm's modern offices on Broad Street every day, one staffer says, "You really know when he is here." Jones and one of his top lieutenants, Donald Woodward, keep tabs on the transactions. But the ten Jones portfolio managers work virtually autonomously with parts of the overall portfolio.

The firm gets new talent by spotting a likely candidate and giving him a "model" portfolio to manage on paper. If he does well, he may even get a small block of capital to work with as a further test. If his performance lags after he is hired, a team of senior managers at the firm gives him informal suggestions. People aren't fired at Jones; they simply don't get any more money to manage. But generally, Jones money managers continue to operate quite independently—unless, of course, they leave to start their own hedge funds.

Jones himself is frankly surprised at how widely his ideas have spread. That may be because making money has been a means, not an end, to him. He appears to be far more interested in things removed from the financial world. Another hedge fund manager recalls that a number of years ago he was invited to a dinner party hosted by Jones, which was attended by about a dozen people. "Most of the conversation was about Yugoslavia," he says. "And it was based on the premise that everyone had been there and had intimate knowledge of what was going on in Yugoslavia. They talked about Yugoslavian affairs, Russian hegemony—all sort of things. I was the only one there who had not been to Yugoslavia."

Indeed, Jones never seems to stray very far from public affairs. One of his latest interests is in conservation. This stems from the fact that he recently had to move from one Connecticut town to another because a freeway project cut through his property. "I've got some bottom land and some upland there," he says, "and I'm working to see what we can do to attract wildlife to the property." When asked about his spare-time activities, he says simply, "My hobby, I suppose, is growing grass." He had a grass tennis court at his old house and will be building a new one.

Why doesn't everyone try to keep up with Jones?

He has thought about that, and figures that the big problem is in selling short. "Some people are not congenitally equipped to sell short," he says. "It goes against their psychological make-up."

He adds that he has "never known any speculator who sold short and didn't hope to make money on it." But the short way of life is more important as a financial insurance policy. With typical understatement, he says, "We hope to lose less on our shorts than we make in offsetting long stocks."

But isn't there a danger of becoming so preoccupied with selling short that buying opportunities are missed?

Not the way A. W. Jones sees it. Just as an understanding of failure is necessary for achieving lasting success, so also can one only truly know an upside market by understanding the downside. "Men who learn to sell short," Jones concludes, "seem to have better judgment on what stocks to buy."

HOWARD STEIN
How to keep the Dreyfus Lion
growling

O
FF WALL STREET, surprisingly few people know who
Howard Stein is. He is not listed in *Who's Who*
("Nobody ever asked me," he explains). He is
rarely interviewed, and he is seldom quoted in periodic financial press roundups of what prominent money managers are
thinking.

The reason is that Stein is the Successor to a Founder, a
position that never seems to fail to produce instant obscurity.
Stein is manager of perhaps the country's second-largest and
probably best known mutual fund, the Dreyfus Fund. Jack
Dreyfus, the fund's founder, is one of the few genuine legends
of Wall Street. The precepts about the market that he devised, and the financial wizardry he employed in propelling
the Dreyfus Fund from $1 million to $310 million in a decade
are still widely discussed.

Dreyfus withdrew totally from the fund eight years ago, and turned it over to Stein, who was immediately branded— and still continues to be thought of as—a caretaker. Stein justifiably feels this assessment is unfair. Under his direction, he points out, "Our assets have grown from $310 million to $2.5 billion. For a caretaker, that's like turning a cottage into a mansion."

Obviously, Stein has been doing something right. Operating in a different fashion from Jack Dreyfus, Stein has tried steadfastly to avoid the encumbering bureaucracy that an organization the size of Dreyfus almost inevitably develops. Not unlike Mr. Johnson at Fidelity Research (p. 95), he has tried to create the kind of free-form atmosphere in which highly talented people can comfortably operate. "The style of management is chaotic," Stein admits. "I am not an organized person. I just kind of like people to be enthused, and excited, and to be able to think freely. I think when you put in too much organization, you hinder the willingness of people to take risks."

Two measures of his success are that the Dreyfus Fund, despite its huge size, has continued to compile an excellent record and that, again like Fidelity, alumni from Stein's antiorganizational system now hold high positions all over Wall Street. Stein's accomplishments in the area of what might be called administrative pioneering flow directly from his own personality, which is unusually instinctive and, for the financial world, quite unconventional.

The words most often used to describe Howard Stein as an investment manager are "intuitive" and "flexible." Two former Dreyfus officers—stretching the same ideas at another angle—have labeled him, respectively, "inarticulate" and "capricious." A present officer of Dreyfus finds him "vague."

At the bottom of all these adjectives lies the indisputable fact that very few people, if any, comprehend the labyrinthine workings of Howard Stein's mind.

Stein is an omnivorous listener who believes that he can learn more from a dialogue than from the printed word. He does not read the painstakingly produced outpourings of the institutional research brokers, for as one colleague states finally, "He doesn't read a bloody thing." Nor is he often swayed by the traditional convincers: numbers. Stein is so unconventional in his approach that his research staff has learned to follow suit. A former vice-president of research said recently, "We never had a traditional research staff. We never had a bunch of guys cranking out a lot of numbers. Howard wants to know what you think in words." Dreyfus has only nine analysts of research. None of them are "technicians" and the group uses no computer, although they do of course subscribe to various services that provide charts and statistical analysis.

Outside the Dreyfus Corp., there are a handful of men on Wall Street with whom Stein has regular telephone sessions and on whom he sounds out his ideas. Stein also likes to talk to people off Wall Street, especially people in government and politics, because he thinks that government exerts vast influence on the market.

In March of 1968, when Stein sensed that Senator Eugene McCarthy's candidacy would effectively galvanize antiwar sentiment, and could lead the Johnson administration toward more direct action to end the war, he took a six-month leave of absence to serve as McCarthy's national finance chairman. Stein personally opposed the war, and important to his decision in helping McCarthy was his belief that the war was taking its toll on the economy and the stock market.

By ear or osmosis, when Stein uncovers an attractive investment idea he uses it as his own (occasionally to the chagrin of its originator) and, more importantly, he acts upon it. Unlike Dreyfus, who analyzed the stock market to uncover a workable set of market-timing theories, Stein operates by no rule book. Two former Dreyfus vice-presidents find it hard to define Stein's investment philosophy, but imply that part of his secret is that he has no investment hang-ups. One says, "Howard is hard to characterize. He is quite a flexible person, and if you provide him with an original peg to hang it on, he'll buy almost anything. Afterwards, if it looks like a bad idea, I've seen him spin on a dime and get out within twenty-four hours." Says another, "The best way to describe Howard's investment thinking is that he is not inhibited."

Stein looks much younger than his age, which is forty-three. Handsome, trim and angular, with pale blue eyes and his dark hair fully intact, he could easily pass for a man in his early thirties. His pictures show a dour and ascetic-looking man, but they are deceiving. Stein's manner with his colleagues is relaxed and easy, his style often humorously self-deprecatory.

Although investment decisions can be made, and are, without Stein's okay, he is rarely more than an arm's length from a dialogue with his colleagues. He uses the telephone often, and so effectively that he goes to his office only three or four days a week.

Outsiders unfamiliar with Stein's habits may still call the Dreyfus switchboard and speak to Stein, without ever realizing that the person on the other end is stretched comfortably in a hammock under the trees behind his 180-year-old French farmhouse in Cross River, N.Y. In the winter, when Stein moves inside, the Dreyfus phone rings in his greenhouse.

Stein's "telephonitis" as his friends call it, is so severe that it allows time for almost nothing else. He does not play golf or cards or tennis, and although his house rests on a ninety-acre plot of woods and ponds and fields, he is not much for walking or tramping through the autumn leaves. His domain is inhabited by his wife and five girls, aged five to fourteen (two are Stein's and wife Janet's; three are hers by a previous marriage), and a mutt menagerie of twenty-six cats and three dogs. The Steins also have a donkey and a gaggle of black and white swans. Nothwithstanding all the parental activity represented by this array, Janet Stein, asked to describe how her husband spends his spare time when he is not on the telephone, responds cheerily, "If you are looking for anything that's off the phone, you can rule it out. He's always on the phone; he likes being close to the action. The only thing I've ever known him to drop the phone for is a good meal."

Though work is Stein's only real hobby, he does enjoy good food. He once commuted to a week's appointments in London from a Paris hotel because he prefers French cooking, but food is his one great extravagance. As a colleague says, "He is not the yacht type."

The man managing $2.5 billion from his hammock was born in Brooklyn on October 6, 1926. His father, who was in the textile business, died when Stein was eight, but not before he and Stein's mother had launched their son on what was almost a career as a violinist. Stein began to practice at the age of five, and when he began grammar school the next year, he says that he outpaced his classmates so quickly that it was decided "it was better I stay home."

So Stein was educated by a teacher who came to his home a few days a week. But most of his day (eight to ten hours, as he remembers it) was spent practicing the violin. Stein now says of his education, "I never went to grade school; therefore I never properly learned to read and write." While this is not, of course, strictly accurate, it is true that Stein eschews the printed word and has difficulty with composition; consequently he writes no memos, and the letters he writes are, he says, "terribly short."

Stein did attend the last couple of years of high school, initially at the private Professional Children's School in Manhattan, which his family couldn't afford for long, and later at a public high school. Afterward, he enrolled at the Juilliard School of Music, and during this period he earned money by selling librettos at the Met. To augment his income, he occasionally stood at the doors after ballet performances and bought back souvenir programs as customers left; at later performances he resold them, thus earning his first capital gains. (A former Dreyfus vice-president, describing Stein's latter-day investment skills, recently observed, "He has a great feel for a depressed situation.")

Then in about 1947, says Stein, "I decided I was never going to be a great violinist, and somehow the idea of being in an orchestra pit didn't appeal to me. So I put the violin in a closet. It's still there, in the same closet. My sister has it." He became a Juilliard dropout, gave up the violin entirely, and today almost never attends concerts or the opera.

If you ask Howard Stein how he was able to give up the violin after devoting virtually his whole life to it, the answer seems typically vague, though apparently not so to him. "It's very easy. You gradually develop a feeling you're a little more interested in something else." It is not too clear what the something else was, although at this point Stein did produce a few off-Broadway shows. One company he formed was called, aptly, Shoestring Productions.

In 1949, when Stein was twenty-three, he got serious about earning a living. He took a $35-a-week job loading steel on trucks for Seaporcel Metals, a Long Island City company with about $2 million in sales. After a year, Stein (who still looks more like a violinist than a steel-handler) was put in charge of personnel. "They took pity on me," he says.

Through Seaporcel executives, who were dabbling in the market, Stein got interested enough in the securities business to venture down to Wall Street, with his paltry credentials, to look for a new job. Not surprisingly, he had little success. But in 1953, through friends of friends, he got a job as a trainee at Bache & Co. Shortly after he made the move, he spotted a stack of mail responses to some Bache retail advertisements lying on a colleague's desk. He began following them up; within six months he had established a substantial business. He is remembered at Bache as a "prodigious worker" who worked so late that his wife (Stein was married in 1952, later divorced, and remarried in 1960) used to come downtown to have dinner with him—"at Horn & Hardart," Stein adds.

As it happened, the market was at the bottom when Stein started at Bache, and his recommendations worked out well. He soon began to hope for a more responsible position, but Bache was reluctant. The attitude was, as he recalls it, "Well, in five years you might work up to assistant manager." In 1955 Stein left for Dreyfus.

Stein went to work for Jack Dreyfus in 1955 in the brokerage firm Dreyfus & Co.; his first move was to set up and run a portfolio management department. Dreyfus was impressed with Stein's performance, and Dreyfus personally controlled both the brokerage house and the Dreyfus Corp., which manages the fund. The fund's net assets at the beginning of 1955 were a mere $2.3 million, but that included, among other good bets, a chunk of a little company called Polaroid. At the end of 1959, a year after the Dreyfus lion first stalked out of the subway and onto the TV screen, the fund's net assets stood at $95 million. The name Dreyfus was fast becoming at once a household word and a legend on Wall Street.

Meanwhile Stein became, as one Dreyfus man puts it, "Jack's alter ego." By 1960 Stein was heavily involved at Dreyfus Corp., helping to invest the fund's money, but in 1962, at thirty-five, he suffered a mild stroke that kept him out of work for six weeks. After Stein recovered, Dreyfus stepped aside and turned the Dreyfus Corp. over to him. Three years later, in 1965, Dreyfus sold most of his stock, the corporation went public, and Stein was named president.

Dreyfus Fund's $2.5 billion net assets are second in size only to those of Investors Mutual, which is a "balanced" fund, with goals of both income and growth. Of twenty-two large growth funds, Dreyfus is almost twice as large as any other fund on the list. Of the eighteen in the group with a record since 1959, only four have shown greater growth in net assets per share than Dreyfus Fund's 243 per cent, and they all are about one-quarter Dreyfus' size or less. On the other hand, twelve of the twenty-one with a record since 1964, have outperformed Dreyfus over that time span.

It is virtually axiomatic that a fund which grows as rapidly as Dreyfus will eventually reach a point where it becomes very difficult to match its former record. The most obvious reality of size is that a large fund, like a fat man, cannot move very swiftly. The old trading techniques are not as useful. Says one Dreyfus man, "Before when we bought 50,000 shares of something and it was a mistake, we knew we could always sell it. Now, when you're buying a million shares, who

are you gonna sell them to?" In a semiannual letter to the
Dreyfus Fund shareholders last year, Stein wrote, "Your fund
might do as well in the next fifteen years as it did in the past,
but it would certainly require a better stock market than we
had before."

Given the new realities of size, it appears that Jack Dreyfus
had remarkable foresight—or luck—when he left the fund's
management and turned it over to Stein. Dreyfus, fifty-six,
is a perfectionist who succeeded to a degree few men can
aspire to in a variety of fields—bridge, gin rummy, golf, horse
breeding, and managing money. As a card player and money
manager he had a professional's feel for the odds. One day in
the late 1940's while intently kibitzing at gin rummy, he
developed an ingenious discard system and ever afterward
has been almost unbeatable at that game.

Dreyfus applied himself in much the same way to figuring
a system to beat the stock market, which he believed was
susceptible to the same probability laws as bridge and gin,
and was also, like cards, influenced by human emotions. One
bullish indicator that he used effectively was an upsurge in
short-selling; in the early 1950's he made his Dreyfus Fund
shareholders lots of money by moving with that indicator to
a large common stock position. Conversely, he liked to con-
vert to cash when, as he put it, "Everybody is bubbly with
optimism and running around telling everyone else to buy,"
which he interpreted to mean "everybody is already fully invested."

If that doesn't sound exactly like a system, well, probably
it wasn't. But it worked. Before the market plunge in October 1957, Dreyfus had only 43 per cent of his fund in common
stocks. By the end of 1957, it was 75 per cent invested.

Dreyfus made his reputation as a market-timing expert

during a period when converting the fund to a 20 per cent cash position meant selling, at the highest, $65 million in stock. Today the comparable figure would be $520 million, and it is difficult to pull that selling maneuver off in a hurry. Recognizing the changes this brings to the management of the fund, one former member of Dreyfus management says, "If Jack were still running the fund, it would be the worst-performing fund you ever saw."

Stein's colleagues find that he is a "wider-ranging person than Jack," less interested in particular stocks or techniques than he is in what they invariably refer to as "concepts"— usually a major long-range development indicated by some government or sociological harbingers.

Beginning in 1967, for example, Dreyfus Corp. put the fund into stocks related to the building industry. Stein embraced the concept but left the decision on which stocks to buy to others. He explains the theory behind this move: "It was really very simple. Vacancy rates were going down and, therefore, there was an abnormal kind of demand." Added to this, Stein foresaw a marked easing of credit with the end of the war in Vietnam.

These factors alone would have made the building stocks a "semi-interesting investment," he says. But Stein now predicts tax incentives and enormous expenditure by government and industry ("comparable to a Vietnam project in size") to provide housing for ghetto dwellers. After this is added to normal demand, the building stocks become an "interesting investment." Stein goes even a step beyond and anticipates that government, in its desire to encourage construction economies, might look favorably on combinations of related companies, such as finance companies and construction companies. Among Dreyfus' largest recent posi-

tions in the building-related field were Flintkote Co., Amer-
ican-Standard Corp., Armstrong Cork, Crane Co., and U. S.
Plywood. The fund's investment in Westinghouse, one of its
dozen largest in a single company, was based in part on
Westinghouse's activity in the home appliance field.

Discussing what may attract him to an individual company,
Stein says, "The genius of a company is very important.
Genius—either inspirational talent or creative talent—builds
a company; not administrative talent. I've never been attracted to an investment where the chief is just a good administrator. A good administrator is important, but he can
only hold the company together."

It is not altogether clear how Stein spots the geniuses, but
it is decidedly not by going out and visiting companies and
getting to know their chiefs. "I find that if I meet with someone and like the person, it tends to handicap my judgment.
How do you meet someone and get to like them, and then tell
them you have to sell their stock in the interest of your shareholders?" asks Stein, as though the problem were insurmount-
able. "You worry you may hurt his feelings and it just gets
too personal."

Stein's visceral way of operating does not always wear well
with his subordinates, and there has been an impressive out-
flow of talent from Dreyfus in recent years. Stein did score
something of a coup when he brought in Robert Price, one of
New York Mayor Lindsay's chief aides, as executive vice-
president at the end of 1966. The two men met during Lindsay's 1965 campaign, which Price managed. They maintained
a telephone dialogue during Price's year as deputy mayor of
New York, and since Price's obsession with the telephone is almost as pronounced as Stein's, the two men got to know each
other very well. When Price's year with the city administra-

tion was up, he moved to Dreyfus as the number two man. The fact that Stein had installed a financial rookie in the second biggest job at the second biggest mutual fund bothered him not at all. "I think you often find more interesting and creative people outside the field," he says flatly. But in 1969, Price left to start his own firm.

Another man who left, Kenneth Oberman, thirty-eight, an immense and pleasant man who was trained as an econometrician and is now director of research for Model Roland & Co., recently explained why: "I am very different from Howard. We have different backgrounds and different personalities. It was very difficult for me to fit mine to his, because the way he would run a mutual fund is different from the way I would run one. Howard is very intuitive; his approach is unique. I'm much more analytical." Oberman nonetheless has great admiration for Stein's ability, and states unequivocally that he has done a "tremendous" job with the fund. Yet, he says with great candor and a touch of wistfulness, "I still think I could run it better." Perhaps the most pervasive criticisms among former employees are of the lack of structure and a clearly defined system of responsibilities. Others complain about Stein's arbitrariness and capriciousness.

Stein recognizes these complaints as having some validity but adds, "We are well-structured where we have to be, in our sales and accounting sections. However, I have always felt that if you have a well-structured organization, you will never be creative."

It is possible that the impressive assemblage of Dreyfus alumni miss the point, that the free and wide-open—perhaps necessarily capricious—atmosphere allowed them to develop their own capabilities and talents. Many able men spend their entire lives in the same company because the bureaucracy is so rigid they never realize how good they really are. One former Dreyfus man acknowledges that "Howard did give me confidence in myself."

Stein feels strongly that while he may lose many good people, his system will also be able to retain its share of good talent, and he has recently been initiating several smaller funds within the Dreyfus organization to give new men even greater authority and responsibility. "When people find out they are effective," he says, "they often want to find an environment where they can make their own decisions." And that is just the kind of environment he intends to continue to provide.

ARNOLD BERNHARD
Merchandising
the astrological approach
to investing

O NE OF THE REASONS for the popularity of astrology is that it appears to bring certainty to an area of maximum uncertainty: the future. While many of us may regard astrological predictions with considerable skepticism at best, it nonetheless takes a hardy person indeed to skip gaily through a day the stars have branded as full of horrendous calamities. We know the prediction is wrong but what if it isn't?

To compare the Value Line organization, publishers of what is perhaps the nation's best-known advisory service, and manager of several very successful mutual funds, with the precepts of astrology is very unfair. Value Line's market predictions are based on far more analysis than that employed by any crystal-ball gazer. However there is one significant parallel: one of the chief reasons for the popularity of the

Value Line Investment Survey is that, like astrology, it appears to really know what is going to happen.

Value Line is basically the personal fiefdom of one man, Arnold Bernhard, a short, hard-driving individual with a moustache and a barely hidden streak of nervous energy. Bernhard's philosophies and theories, which permeate every nook of his organization, stem from the assumption that the future movement of stock prices can be specifically determined by "disciplined analysis" and various formulae based on earnings, dividends and book value. He is so certain about the validity of the formulae that if a stock deviates from where it is supposed to be, it is considered that the *stock* is wrong, and it will be only a matter of time before it slides back to its proper place.

"We impose a discipline on ourselves based on correlation with the past," he says. "This is not infallible, of course, but if a stock has for ten years sold at ten times earnings and this year it is at twenty times earnings without any radical change in the company's business character, which is the moment of insanity? Now? Or the past ten years? If you say the price should be higher, then we say look how much experience you are flying in the face of." "Value Lines" based on cash earnings are then devised, which Bernhard insists correctly predict broad price trends. "If the price was above the line," he says, "it generally goes down to it. If the price was below the line, it goes up to it."

These determinations, along with a multitude of indices and extrapolations, are crammed into one-page summaries of the 1400 stocks which Value Line analyzes regularly. All of the statistics lead up to three basic conclusions. Predictions of how a stock will perform over the next twelve months, and its appreciation potential three to five years hence are ex-

pressed in five categories from I to V. (I is maximum potential to outperform other stocks, and V is least.) Then, as the
coup de théâtre, the survey assigns each stock a "normal average price," a specific dollar figure that it should be selling for,
if it behaves itself, in three to five years.

Arnold Bernhard's distinction is that he was probably the
first to make a broad-scale effort to sell investment information to the public and, most importantly, to employ the techniques of mass merchandising. It had long been obvious to
Bernhard, who once wrote a Broadway column for the *New
York Evening Post* and reviewed theater, music and drama
for *Time*, that such specific predictions would have great
attractions not only to institutions but also to private investors. (Once, a few years ago, the service stopped naming
a specific future price at which stocks should sell. Subscribers,
who no longer were able to compute and make specific
spending plans for capital gains, deluged Value Line with
protests. The predictions soon reappeared.) Now, while there
are currently hundreds if not thousands of advisory services,
none has the following of the Value Line Survey, for which
50,000 subscribers pay $167 a year and which has a renewal
rate upwards of 80 per cent. And none continues to make a
greater effort to promote itself. Financial sections are filled
with ads warning investors not to buy anything until they
have consulted Value Line. Some $2 million is spent on direct
mail solicitations alone.

One of Value Line's most successful promotions has been
its stock market contests. The public is invited by a satura-
tion ad-campaign to enter by selecting from the Value Line
list the twenty-five stocks they think will have the greatest
appreciation over a six-month period. Winners receive cash
prizes of up to $5,000. Meanwhile, until the 1969 contest

Value Line entered its own selection of twenty-five stocks. The reasons for the contest are the following:

1) Hopefully Value Line's list will be shown to have done better than lists from the vast majority of entrants, presumably demonstrating how smart Value Line's system is. (While their list did so perform during the first contest in 1967, it also turned out that, despite the admittedly short period of the test, there was distressingly little correlation between the performance of all 1400 Value Line stocks and their I to V rating. Another problem was the charge that publishing its choices at the start of the contest gave the Value Line list a certain self-fulfillment. The Value Line decided not to enter a list for the 1969 contest.)

2) Entrants, who number in the thousands, hopefully will succumb to the bombardment of subscription solicitations sent them during the contest and for months afterwards.

While all of these tactics have made Value Line Survey an undeniable success, there is wide criticism among professional Wall Streeters of the neatly ordered universe in which Bernhard believes stock prices move. They complain that his view is by far too simplistic. "We subscribe to Value Line, of course," says the head of research of one of the larger brokerage houses, "because we have to know what they are saying to measure impact. But we don't take any of their recommendations." And another contends that "they try to be experts in too many stocks to do a thorough job."

These objections can be at least partially countered by the fact that the Value Line funds have also done extremely well; though, again, critics suggest this is so because the funds don't follow the advice of the survey. One of these funds, the Value Line Fund, designed for growth and income, has in the past decade gained 305 per cent (net assets were $62 million at the end of March 1969), tops in its class over the period. The Value Line Special Situations Fund, led *all* mutual funds over that period, registering a 450 per cent gain (net assets were $361 million at the end of March 1969). The $103 million Value Line Income Fund gained 119 per cent during the ten years.

There is at least one striking contradiction between the funds, which Bernhard manages, and the survey, which Bernhard edits. While the survey has been consistently bearish since the middle 1950's, the funds have been just as bullish, and have been among the top performers in their class.

That may sound like pure investment schizophrenia, yet to Bernhard there is no contradiction. As Bernhard sees it, ". . . the environment is dangerous and stocks as a whole are too high. But among them, some are the best values today."

Thus, Value Line has fairly consistently cautioned its subscribers to be wary and to keep some of their assets in cash for the buying opportunities it sees ahead when stocks decline. At the same time, Value Line funds invest in some favorites from the stocks being watched—most of them listed on the New York Stock Exchange—or pick up the securities of smaller, lesser-known firms not covered by the service.

In 1968, the three Value Line funds were all down in growth in relation to 1967, but they all appreciated. The Value Line Fund appreciated 16.8 per cent versus 68.7 per cent in '67; the Value Line Special Situations 23 per cent versus 106 per cent; the Value Line Income Fund 20 per cent versus 31 per cent. In the Value Line Fund, where the biggest commitments were in electronics and metallurgy, a "real winner" in 1968 was Marcor—which also was included in the portfolio of the Special Situations fund. Martin Marietta, on the other hand, didn't do too well—"it's a transition period for them," says Bernhard. "They're in both building and aerospace, and I think that with peace they'll go more heavily into building." Gulf & Western posted a sizable loss for them in this portfolio, since they bought it at around 50. "Since the end of the year, however," says Bernhard, "we've been adding to our holdings and averaging down the cost. We've also bought others like City Investing and AMK. We're bullish on the conglomerates."

The South African gold stocks did very well in the Value Line Income Fund, which was the fund most heavily in mining, natural gas, and tobacco. The financial and bank stocks did well here too—companies such as CIT, American Credit, Seaboard Finance. One of the big losers in this fund was First National Stores, which they bought for a total of about 1.8 million and watched it drop to 1.5 million. "We're holding it because we're sure someone will eventually take it over," says Bernhard. "We hate to sell it when it's this low."

The Special Situations Fund was most heavily in chemicals, scientific equipment, and computer services. The star performer in this fund was University Computing, which went from $½ million in value to over $21 million. "I think we'll continue to buy it in '69," says Bernhard. "As a matter of fact, we're looking at it very carefully now, since the price has gone down about 50 per cent." City Investing, Occidental Petroleum, Rapid American, Radiation Dynamics and Pennsylvania Life Insurance all did well for Bernhard in this fund. Wheelabrator, on the other hand, "was a real lemon. It was carried long on the enthusiasm for air pollution companies." Molybdenum was another loser for him. "The rare earths just lost their market and we weren't fast enough to see it," admits Bernhard.

For the years ahead, Bernhard says he is "very high on the

savings and loans. I'm betting peace will come, and that they'll be able to slow down the economy. I'm also bullish on the electric utilities." Bernhard explains that although the utilities have been disappointing so far, "they should benefit from the end of high costs and the resulting low interest rates if and when inflation comes down. I also see some increase in rates being approved by regulatory commissions."

To hear Bernhard talk about his success, it all seems to have happened almost by accident. He was born in Hoboken, New Jersey, the son of an immigrant from Germany who sternly indoctrinated him with two bits of fatherly advice: Don't play the horses and don't go near the stock market. After his father died, though, Bernhard's mother began speculating in stocks to build up the small estate she had been left, and Bernhard became interested in the market "vicariously." But Bernhard says he has never played the ponies.

After his brief hitch in journalism, in the late 1920's Bernhard went to work at the office of Jesse Livermore, a noted speculator of the day. His job was in the outside office "as one of the clerks." Bernhard wrote a paper that was bullish on copper stocks in 1928; Livermore "read the paper and sold them all short," he says. "He did not operate on values and I couldn't understand the operation."

Hearing that there was an opening in the railroad department at Moody's, Bernhard next boned up on transportation, "practically memorizing the railroad manual." On the way to his job interview, he was delayed in a subway tie-up, and, being late, ran from the subway to Moody's office. He crashed into a man who was ahead of him and knocked him to the ground. Bernhard became uneasy when they both got off on the seventeenth floor and, sure enough, this turned out to be the man he was to see at Moody's. Yet, after studying a paper Bernhard wrote, the man hired him anyway—"because the lingo was good."

Three years later, in 1931, Bernhard struck out on his own with an investment counseling service. "I had two clients," he recalls, "but as the business grew I had to find some way of analyzing stocks without having a lot of analysts around." Thus, he developed his Value Line concept.

He published his analysis of two hundred stocks in a chart book and began selling it at $200 a copy. But business was slow; his only sale was to the Phipps estate. Finally, Major L. L. B. Angas, who published a service called Diogests, gave Bernhard a rave review and wrote that the service could be had for only $35 a copy. Bernhard was stunned by the price, which was far below what he had been asking. But he quickly did an about-face. "That weekend I got fifty-five checks," he says, "which launched me in the business of publishing a service." An advertisement in a financial magazine and a mailing campaign cemented its profitability.

Today, Value Line has three hundred employees, with seventy analysts and a dozen or so statisticians. But it remains, on the decision-making level at least, pretty much a one-man show. Bernhard keeps tight, almost Napoleonic control over the firm's operations. He alone makes the final decisions on trading the portfolios of the first three Value Line funds, which were started in the early 1950's. "I am head of research, and editor, and manage three funds," he says flatly.

Bernhard adds that "the job is not as difficult as it seems, because all our research is integrated into the rating system." Within this codified system, he explains, the fund manager must "decide how much to buy and how sure you are. Plenty of judgment is involved in picking this stock that is rated 'I' rather than another stock rated 'I.' "

The insulation of most employees from the decision-making level has fed Value Line's reputation as a controversial firm —and has produced a great deal of talent for the competition. Indeed, a surprising number of investors get their analysis from defectors from Bernhard's training ground. He himself admits that his company has lost some 250 analysts to other Wall Street houses. The research vice-president of one smaller firm, who still refers to Bernhard as "The Boss" even though he has been away from Value Line for three years, cites the yen for a bigger pay check and more responsibilities as the reason he left. He also recalls some trying experiences. Once, for instance, an outsider convinced Bernhard to buy the stock of a company this analyst watched. Bernhard didn't even tell him about it. And later, he says, he caught "holy hell" for not figuring on an accounting change that made the company's earnings look better.

Some former employees speak with awe about the way Bernhard is able to attract bright young Phi Betas and turn them into investment pros. "Despite his idiosyncrasies," says another analyst who has moved on into a competing firm, "he is able to get capable, dedicated people who have a great loyalty to the company." Yet even this man complains that "the rating system means you don't need recognized experts."

Bernhard is firmly convinced that a man who watches thirty-five different stocks gets perspective on the market. And he explains the high defection rate by saying that "when you write for Value Line you are under the tyranny of a deadline, so you can't spend as much time looking at a company as you might like." He also suggests that it is difficult to see the follow-through—"that Mrs. Jones bought the stock you recommended."

Still, with his new Development Capital fund, Bernhard has for the first time broadened decision-making at Value Line. This fund is managed by a three-man team, which in the initial stages has included Frank B. Smith, a Value Line veteran who subsequently became president of the Diebold Technology Venture Fund, senior vice-president Louis E. Conham—and, of course, Bernhard himself. It is a closed-end investment vehicle, in the van of the trend toward providing venture capital for extended periods to smaller, emerging companies. As Bernhard explains it, the new fund is a logical extension of the Special Situations Fund, which has had such spectacular successes as its investments in Pacific Plantronics (a $65,000 investment grew to $1.7 million in ten years), and University Computing (after about two years, $495,000 was worth more than $21.3 million).

Value Line analysts, it seems, were turning up more and more potentially profitable special situations—defined, in the shop, as nonrecurring events that change value. But the existing fund was pressing the Securities and Exchange Commission's rule-of-thumb ceiling that limits such restricted investments to 15 per cent of a fund's portfolio. Thus, the Development Capital Corp. was formed in an effort to cash in on these other situations.

For the most part the new fund invests in unregistered letter stock, which it agrees to hold for extended periods. This has three advantages: enabling the fund to buy stock in private companies before they go public; permitting it to take larger positions in emerging companies than it could get by going into the market; and allowing the fund to buy blocks of stock at substantial discounts even when there is a fairly big market for a stock.

With far out—and far off—hopes of return, of course, such investments run real risk of substantial loss. As a result, the fund must look for investments that have inordinately large return possibilities. "Look at it this way," says one Value Line executive. "If you have ten high risk situations, one of the ten has to go up tenfold to offset the possibility of total loss in the other nine. And to put the odds in your favor, every one has to have the prospect of a tenfold gain." A company spokesman sums up the goal: "We invest in development situations. The key word is innovation—in technical things, as they often are."

Innovation is something with which Bernhard has had long experience. For example, he was one of the first men in the investment community to stress the fact that analysts should use earnings estimates for the current year, in addition to considering the previous year's record, in making their forecasts. When he suggested this method some two decades ago, it was radical; some investment men with long memories still consider him something of a maverick, even though this has become standard procedure. And he says that much of Wall Street thought he was "crazy" for projecting bullish postwar earnings even before the Second World War was over.

Bernhard realizes he is a controversial figure, and admits he is a bit "gun-shy" about discussing himself. He knows that many people in Wall Street "say we are wrong and don't follow our ratings." But he suspects that the reason may be that Value Line's low-rated stocks often include some brokerage favorites. "Obviously," he says, "they don't like their customers to be influenced by our ratings."

Bernhard frankly believes that his orderly, disciplined system accounts for his success. He insists that the Value Line approach would bring "superior results no matter which man in our organization was running the funds, providing he had been indoctrinated in our methods."

So, when he is asked what groups of stocks he favors, Bernhard has a pat answer. "Whatever the kind of market we're in," he says, "I like groups that are in the top ten of Value Line's weekly summary index. Recently these included . . ."

At sixty-seven, Arnold Bernhard sports a deep suntan, acquired on the tennis court at his Westport, Conn., home, where he plays avidly on weekends. He also owns an island in the Bahamas called Hummingbird Cay, where he is building a biological research laboratory.

Like many Wall Street money managers, however, Bernhard has not had an especially high batting average when he has branched out into other areas. Some years ago, he financed the ambitiously erudite Mid-Century Book Club, which numbered Jacques Barzun among its editors, but the club folded after a few relatively unsuccessful years. He once wrote a play about the stock market; it was never produced. And his record as a Broadway "angel" has been equally unfortunate. Ever since a big success with *Never Too Late*, he has had nothing but a string of failures. This has been a major disappointment. His early experience as a theater critic led him to believe "I'd be pretty good at it," Bernhard says wistfully, "but I have picked more losers than winners."

Fortunately for Bernhard, he spends most of his time looking at Wall Street.

THE MISSIONARIES 3

Introduction

CONSIDERING THE AMOUNT of public attention that is focused on mutual funds, it is not surprising that stars should flourish.

And considering the performance derby, it is also not surprising that these funds should be managed with the greatest venturesomeness and aggressiveness. But the great bulk of money in institutions—banks, pension funds, endowment funds, foundations—is insulated from public scrutiny and fiercely competitive pressures. There are therefore no stars in these institutions, and changes in the more traditional methods of money management are slow in coming.

The men in this section are missionaries, eagerly carrying the new mutual fund performance tenets to the hinterland of more staid institutions. *John Bristol* and *Roland Grimm* are helping universities to alleviate some of their urgent financial troubles by increasing the return on their endowment portfolios. *Vernon Eagle* is proselytizing the foundations, repositories of especially lugubriously-managed money. He feels that foundations should be just as interested in the betterment of their portfolio yield as they are in the betterment of man. *John Hartwell* and his investment counseling firm are providing adventurous, well-organized management to a host of private accounts, ranging from pension funds and endowment funds to individual trusts.

Perhaps the most significant missionary is *Carl Hathaway*, who at thirty-four is working to modernize those institutions which have traditionally been the most steadfast advocates of the status quo, the banks. Banks today do not exactly swing, but their sizable loss of investment management business to firms such as Hartwell's and Bristol's has caused them to modernize and hire men like Hathaway. Tall, lean and hard, Hathaway looks like a traditional young banker. But his ideas are probably somewhat disquieting to old-timers, especially since he is directly responsible for the investment of $9 billion dollars. "Change is a way of life," he says. "If you cannot adjust to this fact you will be mediocre. I am not bound by tradition or anything else. Investment managers who cannot change will perish."

CARL HATHAWAY
Go-go kid
at the House of Morgan

"**D**o not invest in companies run by fat men. Corporations usually represent the characteristics of their chief executive, and fat designates lack of self-control. I like lean, hard, ambitious managements."

The originator of this interesting investment maxim is a lean, hard and ambitious man named Carl Hathaway who manages over $9 billion worth of securities. He is sitting near the center of a large wood-paneled room occupied by forty desks and thirty-nine other men, each precisely dressed in a dark-blue suit and black shoes. All of the men are reposing quietly in leather armchairs. All of the desks are shined, and have roll-tops and adjoining carved antique cabinets. The room houses part of the investment department of the Morgan Guaranty Trust Co.

There are two distinctive things about Hathaway. One

is that next to *his* desk is a small, carved, nineteenth-century buffet cabinet. It is the only such item of furniture in the room and an immediate sign, to those attuned to the nuances of corporate status, that he is in charge of the thirty-nine others. The other distinctive thing about him is that, though he is only thirty-four, he happens to supervise directly the purchase and sale of more common stock than anyone else in the country.

Despite his superannuated office accoutrements, Carl Hathaway personifies the new, tough breed of investment manager now assuming increasingly large responsibilities at the nation's banks long known for their hidebound, ultra-conservative approach to money management. For the past two years, it has been Hathaway's responsibility to oversee all equity investments made by that part of Morgan's investment department that manages pension funds. Assets in pension accounts total over $9 billion, about 65 per cent of which is in common stocks. In 1968 the Morgan pension group bought about $1.3 billion worth of common issues and sold $700 million worth.

Hathaway formally operates "within the parameters" of the trust committee of several senior Morgan executives. In other words, if he or one of his own managers working on a specific group of accounts should decide that a major change in several pension accounts should be made, Hathaway must obtain the approval of a majority of the trust committee's members. However, this procedure is surprisingly uncumbersome: if necessary, a decision can be forthcoming within minutes. Hathaway, in addition, has charge of two house funds in which pension funds may invest: a fixed-income fund which contains debt and preferred securities with provisions for conversion into common stock; and an aggressive common stock fund. Finally he manages from thirty to fifty corporate pension trusts, among them some of the largest at the bank.

Vesting all this responsibility in a single man—allowing one man to plot one strategy for all of its pension accounts' equity investments—is extremely unusual, especially for a bank with the size and prestige of Morgan Guaranty. Traditionally, trust accounts have been spread widely among many dozens of individual managers, with little attempt at the organization of a central strategy. The feeling was that putting a single person in control might be dangerous and unstable; that maximum safety and protection lay in diffuse, widely apportioned responsibility.

The reason for this move, according to senior V. P. Harrison Smith, one of Hathaway's two immediate bosses who thought up the job, is that "since pension funds are in the same legal and technical situations, and have the same exemptions from taxes, the same constant cash flow, and the same long-term goals, they're more homogeneous than other types of accounts. It's possible to centralize the buying of equities."

The main reason, though, is that magic word "performance." When Harrison Smith discusses this point, he sounds like the manager of any swinging mutual fund. He says that the system allows the portfolios to be more concentrated: one third of the money in only ten stocks, another third in forty stocks and the rest spread widely. Selling can be more systematic, and bad stocks can be quickly weeded out. "You can't afford the luxury of holding stocks simply because the companies are well regarded, just as the Army can no longer afford to have a cavalry, although it would be nice."

These sentiments and the fact of Hathaway's job typify the rapid shift in the philosophy of investment management at many of the nation's banks. In the old days, banks reigned supreme as investment managers. Anyone—individuals, corporations, foundations, pension funds—with money to be managed had to take it to a bank because that was the only prudent and safe thing to do. And at the banks, asset management was usually left to graying men who felt their chief duty was to protect against theft and embezzlement and keep the money in government bonds with the highest yield.

In the past decade or two, those with money to be managed—college endowment funds, foundations, pension funds, private individuals—have come to realize that wise investment in common stocks, convertible bonds and other more venturesome equities could significantly raise return with only a minimal sacrifice in safety. Independent investment counselors have become increasingly aggressive, and go-go mutual funds have flourished. Both have begun to relieve the banks of a significant portion of their investment business. Banks are not noted for their rapid shifts in policy, and many bank executives at first refused to be swayed by what they viewed as the glandular vibrations of young hippies. Yet now almost all banks have begun policies to demonstrate they are as capable of aggressive money management, if the circumstances call for it, as anyone else. One might guess that the banks most resistant to change would be the huge cumbersome behemoths. In reality, the Morgan Guaranty Bank, with more trust assets ($17 billion) under its control than any other bank in the U.S. has been one of the most enthusiastic devotees of modern techniques.

One of the results of this is Carl Hathaway. Hathaway is almost uniquely suited to his position because he bridges the gap between old banking and new banking by combining an aggressive and imaginative approach to investing with a traditional devotion to such comfortable (to traditional senior bank executives) precepts as hard work, self-control and self-discipline. "He has a kind of controlled intelligence that is very unusual in this business," remarks a fellow executive. "Others are always flying very high or very low, but Carl stays calm and deliberate."

Hathaway is a sharply chiseled man who looks like he might be made out of very hard rubber. His cheeks are always bright red, as if he had just jogged down from his commuter train at Grand Central. (He *does* ride a fire-engine-red Honda to the Darien, Conn., station at the other end.) He sits draped lithely over the arms of his swivel chair. When he peers over the top of his glasses as he talks, he looks like an eleven-year-old playing a grandfather in a school play. He talks slowly and deliberately, never going back to change a word or modify a thought.

Listen to some of his statements, which, it is clear to the listener, are not idle platitudes expressed for the benefit of the public but deeply held beliefs:

"What you achieve on Wall Street is directly related to your ability, and how hard you work. Lazy people bore me. The most successful of my friends remind me of a 727 at takeoff: full throttle and straight up."

"I was awed by the first million I managed, but I got used to it. If you're afraid of dealing with large amounts of money, you won't be able to make decisions. In this business, you cannot be weak-kneed or wishy-washy."

At the same time Hathaway makes remarks like this:

"Change is a way of life. If you cannot adjust to this fact, you will be mediocre. Investment managers who cannot change will perish."

"My philosophy of investing money is this: I am not bound

by tradition or anything else. Often that means I will be alone if I feel that is the best course to follow."

"I am not a political animal. I do things because I have conviction. I will speak up or do something unpopular. By nature I am not a compromiser; I am not cut to please the greatest number. I am out to do the best job possible."

While the last three statements might be expected to stir a measure of disquiet in a bank the size of Morgan Guaranty, Hathaway's first two remarks engender his superiors' confidence. He was chosen for the job, says Morgan senior V.P. Samuel Calloway because the top executives were impressed with his "crisp, succinct" command of facts, his ability to use them persuasively and his thorough research.

Hathaway's relationship with his inferiors (and outsiders as well) tends to be, in the words of some, "laconic," "without pleasantries." Adds one associate, "Carl tends to have a slightly disruptive influence on other departments." A former research department member comments, "The whisper would go through the department, 'Here he comes,' and everybody would quake." Hathaway is no more jaunty with outsiders, especially institutional salesmen from brokerage houses, too many of whom, he complains, ". . . call me up to tell me what's in *The Wall Street Journal* that morning. I can read too."

"When Carl goes down to the research department to find out something, he's not going down to play games," adds Calloway. "He gives the impression of great vitality, which is another way of saying he is aggressive in a nice way." As a supervisor, Calloway continues, "Hathaway is direct, clear, easy to get along with. People know where they stand with him."

Among the swingers of Wall Street, who generally have a well-articulated disdain for the staid mustiness of most bank investment managers, Hathaway commands considerable respect. "I can't think of anyone at any bank I'd rather have handle aggressive money for me," says one. He has as broad a circle of friends outside the banking business as many hedge fund managers. One older Morgan executive, who terms him "our liaison with the underground," adds, "He certainly is a fast-moving guy. I'm sure he wouldn't have the patience for the long negotiations involved in, say, lease-backs."

Hathaway's philosophy of investing, if not startlingly iconoclastic, is straightforward and logical.

He believes foremost in a "conceptual approach": "First I look for a need in the society. Then I look for the industries that are going to fill that need, then for the companies that will fill that need most profitably." At the present time, he says, "a socio-economic revolution is being precipitated in the cities, and the government is being forced to redirect a big flow of assets into urban development." The resulting investment opportunities will be not just in the construction industry, but especially in the more profitable ancillary industries such as plumbing fixtures, he feels. Other industries he favors are: information technology, computers, office equipment, publishing, household products, food and beverage, and metals and coppers.

He believes in companies that have "an international franchise, usually a unique product but sometimes a unique claim to natural resources or something similar." Companies he puts in this group are: Xerox, Kodak, Coca Cola, Gillette, IBM.

He believes in concentration: "Too many stocks means one of two things: You don't know how to pick them or you have no sense of timing."

He believes in technology: "Never before the present has there been such a great possibility that research and development will produce new industries—whole new industries that didn't exist a decade ago."

He believes in turnover: "If your money goes up 100 per cent, it doesn't go up as much as if you'd bought five companies successively and sold each out when it had gone up 20 per cent. With the latter method you start from a bigger base each time."

He believes in following price action closely: "I am an avid reader of charts, and I tell the people who work with me to watch daily price changes to develop a feel for a stock's and the market's behavior. Most days I take an hour or so to read every single price change on the big board."

He does not believe in relying on a lot of outside advice: "If you don't have the background, you have to rely on what other people tell you. But if you do you'll be wrong."

There are limits to what he can do in some of these areas, however. Concentration, for instance, will always be hampered by the arrival of new accounts which usually bring with them as many as fifty stocks the bank doesn't own and doesn't really want to own. However, as Harrison Smith says, "We can't make sales just for the sake of neatness." Still, Hathaway has been able to make considerable headway in paring down many of the new accounts.

While the turnover in Morgan's pension fund equity investments is 10 to 15 per cent annually—five times that of the average bank—Hathaway makes clear he is not indulging in speculative trading. "We don't sell stocks just to take a profit or because they're too high or low," he says. The only time we sell is when the fundamentals surrounding the industry or the company's profitability have changed for the worse."

One of Hathaway's principal precepts is "the whole world around you is an investment spectrum"; that useful information may come from very unlikely sources. He does a great deal of general reading. "I go so far as to read *Glamour* magazine to find out, say, how a cosmetic company is presenting itself to the market," he says. "If I see five pages of advertising for Clairol, then I know Bristol-Myers is making an aggressive effort to keep its share of the market or improve it."

Hathaway, in fact, is interested in communications in a broad sense. He defines communications as "things that bring people together." He feels companies in such fields as photography, television and office equipment (all communications, by his definition) offer excellent investment opportunities. Another example would be the hair dye manufacturers. Bristol-Myers, again, created a need for hair-coloring by making it respectable. "It used to be that if you obviously dyed your hair you got taken off in a paddy wagon. Now there is a lot of dyed hair on ladies in sub-urban houses surrounded by white picket fences." How is dyed hair communications? "It's not verbal communications," he answers, "but it is communication through appearance and through the awareness of appearance." Hathaway puts liquor companies in the communications area because they help blur appearance: "One of the ways our society functions is through the cocktail party, and alcohol allows people to talk to each other."

Companies Hathaway looks at least are those that are not

masters of their own destiny, those operating within strict regulation, or subject to natural catastrophes. He dislikes industries, such as the railroads, whose technology is not advancing. He stays away from industries, such as paper and steel, which increase their capacity in a static market but do not generally bolster their prices.

One of Hathaway's main contributions at Morgan Guaranty has been to establish, for the first time, specific guidelines for pension fund managers to follow in selecting stocks. He regards himself as a kind of "catalyst," assimilating ideas and opinions from a wide variety of sources, and then codifying them into specific dicta. For the bank's aggressive Special Situations Investments Equity fund, he set forth five criteria for a good purchase:

1) Managerial competence and integrity, identified through competitive checks as well as through other sources.

2) Competitive advantage from a unique managerial concept or unique product.

3) Fifteen per cent compound annual earnings growth.

4) Market value doubling five years after purchase.

5) An above-average return in capital and common equity or a marked improvement in them.

Between November 1964, when Hathaway reorganized the fund, and April 1969, the fund increased 161 per cent, against an 8.6 per cent rise in the Dow Jones Industrial Average.

In 1967, the fund increased 69 per cent. Only seventeen mutual funds over $10 million did this well during the same period, and no mutual fund anything like the size of SSIE ($123.1 million on September 30, 1967) did as well.

It was less than ten years ago that Hathaway decided to work in a bank. After high school in his native Brookline, Mass., where his father ran a chain of restaurants and coffee shops, he went to Harvard. At the time he was considering medicine, until, he says, "I ran into integral calculus and bio-chemistry while I was playing a lot of hockey. The deans politely told me that I had better choose between them or I wasn't going to be there very long." He chose hockey and a major in government. "The only economics I had," he remembers, "was Samuelson's 'Guns and Butter' [Harvard's basic economics course]." Shortly before he left school, a guidance counselor asked if he would like to work in a bank and he replied that was the last thing he wanted to do.

He graduated from Harvard in 1955, and after a two-year stretch in the Navy he came to realize that while his liberal arts education had taught him "how to think," it had left him "still young and untutored." He thought about his eco-nomics course and saw that an undeniable advantage of the business world was never only one alternative. "Everything wasn't clear-cut. It involved a lot of curiosity and I saw that what I liked best was to look into something and see what really made it tick."

He decided to enroll in Cornell Business School, and as he became steadily more wrapped up in the case studies of com-panies, he felt strongly that he had made the correct decision. In 1959, he joined Morgan's research department, where he covered drugs, chemicals, nonferrous metals, and the tire and rubber companies. In 1961, he was assigned to the in-vestment department, where he rose rapidly to his new position.

In the new job his routine has remained more or less the same: the 6.02 from Darien, where he lives with his wife and three sons; in the office by 8:30; out of the office by 5:30. He spends about two evenings a week in town for meetings. He is finding himself spending more time with the bank's potential

trust customers because Morgan has no institutional salesmen—"We don't need a group of trained seals that go
around with charts and sell the bank's services," he says.

On weekends, continuing his college interest, Hathaway
likes to play hockey with the suburban Winter Club Ice
Hockey League. (He even tried out for the Olympic Team
when he was in the Navy.) Sports, hockey especially, he
feels, help him with his job: "There's pressure and a great
desire to win. It helps keep up the competitive instinct."

In assessing the future, Hathaway admits he has been
lured, like so many of his other young and capable banking
colleagues, by some of the swinging mutual funds, where one
typically gets a "piece of the action" as well as other more
spiritual rewards. One fund man guesses Hathaway could
easily triple his salary on the outside. Hathaway says loyalty
is one big reason he has stayed at Morgan: "They've given a
lot to me and I've given a lot to them." Yet a very significant
reason is simply the sheer stimulation provided by the huge
pile of stock he runs, and the considerable freedom he has
in running it.

"The biggest challenge in this business is being early," he
says, "and the bigger you are the earlier you have to be.
If you are small you can catch up more easily. Your reaction time can be a little late. But if you are big you have
to be first." The size of this responsibility sharpens for Carl
Hathaway, brings to a keen needle point, what he sees as
the "key element of success": "To go against the grain, to
be out by yourself."

JOHN HARTWELL
Beating the star system
through organization

S OME MEN WORK with their jackets on, a style of office attire that tends to indicate they are operating in a slow, rather restrictive working environment. Other men work with their jackets off, their collars unbuttoned and their tie knots loosened. This usually indicates a free-wheeling, hard-working, creative, but perhaps a bit uncontrolled type of atmosphere. A third group of men remove their jackets but carefully leave their collars and ties neatly in place, which signals that a certain tight efficiency has been successfully blended with unfettered industriousness.

This little parcel of probably oversimplified psychological theorizing is by way of introduction to a money manager named John M. Hartwell. He is a tall, lean, ship's captain-type of fifty-two years, with close-cropped sandy hair. He speaks forcefully and deliberately yet with an unexpected offhand good humor, especially when he is being iconoclastic. It is impossible to visualize him working either with a coat on, or his tie loosened.

Hartwell's firm, J. M. Hartwell & Co., manages two public mutual funds with assets of $100 million. But his most important business is investment counseling of private accounts which total some $325 million.

As was noted in the previous chapter, independent investment counselors, by applying the performance strategies of the aggressive mutual funds to the management of private accounts, have been able to steal much business from bank trust departments. That the investment counselors were able to realize this opportunity is due in no small part to the example set by John Hartwell. In many senses, Hartwell qualifies as a pioneer as much as a missionary. Not only did he develop many important performance concepts, but he helped initiate such practices as public disclosure of his private accounts' performance, and insistence by the advisor on complete discretion over the accounts.

John Hartwell is not a star, a solitary soul attempting to get in tune with the ethereal waftings of market emanations, like Fred Alger or Dave Meid. He is just as aggressive as the latter two men. Indeed he is just as thoroughly possessed with a passion to beat the market, to beat the competition. But his method of doing so is quite different. Let's use a rough analogy. Asked their idea of a military attack, Alger and Meid might talk about loading up with pocketfuls of grenades, a machine gun, a couple of pistols, and then making a loud, wild dash at the enemy: "Banzai! Over the top!" and so forth. Hartwell, on the other hand, would speak in terms of launching a Normandy Invasion.

"Performance can be maintained for a short period by

unique talents or good fortune," he asserts. "But over a long period it can be attained only by superior organization. This is why long-term performance is so infrequently realized. One must *organize* for it." This means identifying the characteristics that have produced the good performance, avoiding any extraneous elements that will interfere with concentrated attention on the necessary procedures, and seeking to maximize the use of all the necessary steps. In other words, Hartwell isn't trying just to win a few battles. He wants to win the war.

In order to put together this sort of organization, Hartwell has hired a number of the best young portfolio managers he could find—most are in their mid-thirties—and he has given them maximum authority and responsibility for specific accounts. He has established a generous incentive compensation system to reward them when they do well and penalize them when they don't. Hartwell readily acknowledges that many of the best portfolio men "hate organization." Therefore he has tried to keep his men laboring happily under the same roof, freely exercising their initiative, by declining to burden them with second-guessing and lots of organized work procedures.

A second step has been to remove his clients from the process as much as possible. After an initial conference to ascertain their investment objectives—"aggressive," "conservative," or "income" (almost all of his accounts are "aggressive" with maximum emphasis on capital gains)—he then invites them, in effect, to make themselves scarce. He insists they give him total "discretion": carte-blanche authority to invest their money where and when he sees fit. If they don't like what he is doing, they are free to take their money elsewhere.

"It's not that we want to be hard-boiled," Hartwell says,

"but when we decide after considerable deliberation to take a position in a company we don't like to be told by the client, for instance, that he had a bad experience with the stock a few years back." If, as happens on rare occasions, a client insists with sufficient vehemence on having his money in a certain stock, Hartwell may accede to the request. But he will then transfer the purchase funds totally out of the client's discretionary account and segregate the acquired shares in a separate category. Hartwell's performance record for that account will thus not be sullied by haphazard, ill-advised inputs.

Hartwell's investment philosophy is just as ruthlessly delineated. To begin with, he avoids excessive diversification in his portfolios. "If you have more than half a dozen positions in an account of, say, $500,000, it can only mean that you're not sharp enough to select real winners." In picking real winners, Hartwell is a staunch fundamentalist. He believes that while general market conditions, psychology, technical factors and so on are important, the movement of stocks is basically determined by the progress, or lack thereof, of their earnings. The response of the former to the latter is rapid: "When a good situation develops, it gets noticed fast. Nothing sits around waiting for action."

Sometimes the earnings rise will be the result of a turn-around in operations. The classic example of an ailing company which was suddenly transformed into a healthy one was Chrysler. Hartwell bought heavily in the spring of 1962 just as the change—the result of new management—was being realized on Wall Street; he later sold in early 1965 near the high. More recently, in 1969, Hartwell has been in a turnaround situation with Marcor, the amalgam of Montgomery Ward and Container Corp., which has experienced a remarkable earnings revitalization and an accompanying appreciation in its stock.

But more often profit rises will come from changes in the economic and business environment which favor certain groups. The computer software companies, which benefited from the new generation of computers, are good illustrations. Some of Hartwell's current favorites in 1969 are firms specializing in selling land, such as Horizon, AMREP and Deltona. "It may be because these companies are doing an increasingly excellent sales job," he says, "but the fact is that with inflation continuing more and more people are becoming aware of real estate values and are putting their money in land."

Hartwell sees the construction field as an equally big growth area and he figured out that the best way to participate in it is through purchase of mortgage investment trusts. Tight money conditions have made it extremely difficult for construction companies to finance their building projects. The mortgage investment trusts raise money through public security and debt offerings, then lend it to builders at substantial interest rates. After the construction is finished, the firms are paid off and the mortgage is passed to more conventional holders. "This is an entirely new kind of business which seems to fill a real need," he says. "We have positions in seven of these companies and the oldest one, Associated Mortgage Investors, is only a year old."

Hartwell's purchasing in these two groups brings us to his theory of market timing. The market in 1968 and at least through the middle of 1969 was weak, a situation Hartwell feels, during which it is possible to make some worthwhile portfolio switches, because downswings "may mark the end of some stocks and the beginning of others."

He explains the process this way: "A market boom [such as 1967] inevitably produces excesses, overpriced groups, overly high prices. When a shakeout comes—ten per cent or so— there is an inherent tendency to take a second look at your holdings, take a cold shower so to speak, and probably take some profits. This means that the favorites get hit hard and people start looking around for new groups whose values haven't been appreciated."

Taking advantage of this realignment and getting into the new groups involves some good selling which, Hartwell maintains, is much more difficult than good buying. One must avoid becoming emotionally involved with his holdings and realize that "Stocks are only pieces of paper." Some parts of the portfolio which should be sold may be down badly from their purchase price. "It can be difficult selling them," he says, "but you simply have to realize that many of them just are not going to come back." If a stock has had a good rise, one should not allow his "enchantment" with its success to detract from a hard determination that "its prospects for future appreciation are substantially diminished." One must "reap the harvest before it spoils."

The formulation of theories is always easier than their execution, of course. What has Hartwell's record been? The 1967 performance of Hartwell's Hartwell and Campbell Fund was excellent: up 80.3 per cent against a gain in the Dow Jones Industrial Average of 15 per cent. Indeed the Hartwell record during the late 60's may well be unassailable. As of July 31, 1968, "aggressive" accounts he has had for four and a half years had appreciated an average of 259.7 per cent against a rise in the Dow of 10.3 per cent. His oldest current account, which he has had for six and a quarter years, is up 517.5 per cent against a mere 26.7 per cent on the Dow.

In 1968, however, the Hartwell and Campbell Fund (and most of his other private accounts which generally own many of the same issues), like many other mutual funds in the capital-gains-oriented category, did relatively poorly. Against a 4.3 per cent rise in the Dow, it was up only 13.5 per cent, less than the average for all mutual funds. During the first few months of 1969, the fund was down twice as much as the Dow.

Hartwell attributes these results in part to the historical fact that his accounts always way outperform the Dow on the upside; but concomitantly do worse on the downside. He is always trying to stay in those stocks—many are small, new companies Over-the-Counter—which appear to have the greatest upside potential, he explains, but "when the market goes down those stocks are often judged as 'unseasoned' and they get hit harder than other stocks. We try to run aggressive portfolios and this means volatility in both directions. But remember: the market moves up much more than it moves down."

Nevertheless, Hartwell admits he made some major misinterpretations of the market favorites in 1968. At the beginning of the year, he found himself still invested in two groups which had already topped out and which had begun to experience some stiff selling pressure: conglomerates and office equipment companies—the latter especially, he says, had been "overexploited." Though he admits he "took a real bath," he at least got out of these groups as quickly as he could once he realized his mistake, and many of these stocks were later to go much lower. "After this bad start—we were down 20 per cent during the first quarter—we had to spend the rest of the year catching up."

Though Hartwell picked up stocks in one of the new vogue

groups that developed—franchising—he missed two of the other favorites: mobile homes and nursing homes. "Practically nobody really anticipated how good the earnings of the mobile homes would be," he recalls. "Just a short while ago I looked in our files for reports we had received on these companies in 1967 and I can truthfully say that on the basis of those reports I still wouldn't have bought any of them."

Despite these misses, Hartwell does not question one of his principal organizational theories: lack of a research staff. He feels that the market and the kinds of interesting stocks change so rapidly that it is senseless to attempt to assemble a staff that will be expert in all the necessary areas. He relies instead on outside analysts at the brokerage houses—when real estate stocks appear to be a good buy he is then free to go to whomever the best real estate man may be and solicit his views.

"It would be foolish to duplicate the work of these men even if anyone could," he contends. "What we do is take the best research Wall Street has to offer, distill it, evaluate it and act on it." His reliance on outsiders is so complete that he makes no attempt to visit or even contact the management of companies in which he invests. "There's no point in getting involved in company visits unless you have the time to carry out a consistent program, which we obviously don't."

Hartwell works off and on with a total of perhaps eighty brokerage houses, though only a handful of houses—or more likely a handful of analysts with a particular house—will be "hot" and "in phase" with the market at any particular moment. Like most other investment advisors, he rewards with commission business those brokerage houses that assist him; the considerable size of the assets he manages means that many good ideas are brought to him first. (Not all good information works out salubriously. In late 1968 Hartwell's firm was one of those charged by the SEC with having received "inside" information from Merrill Lynch in 1966 on a sudden decline in the earnings of Douglas Aircraft. The case has not as yet been resolved.)

Much good information these days comes from regional brokerage houses in Denver, Minneapolis, Atlanta and the like which, unlike New York firms, are able to stay apprised of the hundreds of small but exciting companies that have been going public. "These firms get out and find more than their share of interesting situations," Hartwell says.

He is not satisfied with hearing a good story from one analyst, however. "We invariably go to someone else to verify a story," he says, "and we keep moving around until we have fully satisfied ourselves that the situation is something we ought to be in. And if something goes wrong with the stock, we want to have more than one contact we can fall back on, who can quickly telephone someone influential in the company and find out what is going on."

Searching out hot stocks is a profession Hartwell arrived at only after some uncharacteristically disorganized wanderings through a number of other jobs. He grew up in Somerville and Belmont outside Boston, where his father was a builder, then went to Harvard where he graduated cum laude in economics in 1936. He felt finance was clearly his field, and he proceeded to Harvard Business School. After leaving the B-School he worked, variously, as an economics and accounting instructor at Rutgers and MIT; a salesman for an accounting service for Union Carbide; a Naval Officer during the Second World War; an economics analyst for Mutual of New York; an economist for Ford; a venture capitalist in

Santa Barbara; treasurer of the Piedmont Life Insurance Co.—all before finally ending up at his first really significant post: president and director of Piedmont Advisory Corp., investment advisors for the wealthy Smith Richardson family (repository of much of the Vick Chemical fortune).

This was not Hartwell's style, however. Decidedly a creature of the urban Northeast, he was forced to live in Greensboro, N.C. Members of the Richardson family, moreover, were something less than vigorous in their conception of investment. After four and a half years, Hartwell quit. "They wanted conservative appreciation and it bored me," he says. In 1959, he went to work for Imrie de Vegh, the brilliant, capricious founder of the de Vegh mutual fund. "You could hardly name a company he didn't know inside out," Hartwell remembers. "He could regale you on any company for hours. He could take a fifty-five-year-old lady who didn't know what a stock was and talk to her about Southern Pacific for an hour and she'd think it was as interesting as *Hello, Dolly!*"

The fast pace at de Vegh finally provoked Hartwell into doing something he had been cogitating about for twenty years without daring to leap: starting his own business. He left de Vegh in December 1961 and opened his own investment counseling firm. The time was not especially auspicious for such a move: it was the height of the bull market before the 1962 break. "I had no accounts," he says, "just ambition and a six-month contract with a mutual fund."

He did well enough for his initial clients, however, that he was soon recommended to others. One of his best early thoughts came in 1963 after he noticed a *New York Times* ad promoting an article in the *Reader's Digest* about birth control pills. He decided to buy one of the few companies supplying that market, a small firm by the name of Syntex which was selling at 36. A year later he sold out at 200, a profit that was not hard to take even though heavy performance-fund buying was to send the price rocketing incredibly higher.

In addition to the Hartwell and Campbell Fund, he also advises the recently initiated Hartwell and Campbell Leverage Fund (which already has over $60 million in assets). His office, clean, modern, and metallic, looms forty floors above Park Avenue and is decorated with abstract lithographs and etchings. He and his wife—two children are away at school—own a home in Greenwich, Conn., but he maintains an apartment on Sutton Place where he stays most week nights. As is true of many other aggressive fund managers, his outside interests are negligible—he gets up and goes to bed with the market. (He did at one time invest in a Broadway play entitled *How to Make a Million*. It didn't, and was Hartwell's last theatrical venture.)

While he enjoys participating in the performance fund sweepstakes with the youngsters, Hartwell is convinced that over the long term his business will tend more and more toward private investment counseling. "We're bringing in new business in good $10 million and $20 million chunks all the time. We wouldn't be able to match that with the mutual fund even if we had the Enterprise Fund's record."

While he once concentrated on accounts of private individuals, many of his new accounts are such once-quiescent pools of capital as foundations, union pension funds and university endowment funds—all of which are beginning to understand the delights and benefits of superior investment results. Hartwell assists them in this understanding with a formidable sales and marketing force, abristle with handsome brochures filled with Hartwell's past record. Hartwell's firm, in fact, is one of the few to publish publicly audited performance results of his various accounts (identified, of course, only by number). A more abstract selling tool, but equally effective, is the quiet, calm confidence that Hartwell exudes, which tends to give potential clients the impression that somehow his portfolios of tiny OTC companies, swinging new technology firms and other possibly swiftly zipping movers are as safe and secure as good old IBM.

"Five years from now," says Hartwell, "the days of the really well-known fund managers will be gone. The incredible compensation scale is going to draw a huge number of able people into this field." The stars will rise and fall, with increasing rapidity. The Hartwell organization, he expects, will endure.

JOHN BRISTOL
Bringing performance
to the campus

"WE HAVE A REPUTATION for listening to unusual investment ideas."

While that may seem like a statement from the manager of a small aggressive hedge fund, it was really made by a man on whose judgment of the market many of the most prestigious colleges and universities in the country depend. The man is John W. Bristol, whose investment counseling firm advises such schools as Princeton, Swarthmore, Colby, Howard, the University of Miami and many others on the investment of their endowment funds. Along with Roland Grimm (see p. 189), Bristol has been instrumental in convincing university trustees that by abandoning the ultraconservative policies that have dominated endowment fund management, and instituting in their place an aggressive emphasis on achieving maximum return, the schools can help alleviate the serious financial bind in which most of them find themselves.

The firm that is now Bristol's was founded more than thirty years ago to handle college funds. It went through a couple of name changes and owners, finally becoming John W. Bristol & Co., Inc., after Bristol bought out his partner, the late Paul B. Wyant, who went off in 1954 to become treasurer of Scott Paper Co.

Bristol graduated in 1935 from Williams College, worked in two Wall Street firms, then took a job with the investment manager of the Phipps estate in 1938, helping to manage a fortune which arose from its founder's association with Andrew Carnegie in U.S. Steel. In 1943 he entered the Army Air Force. When the war ended, instead of going back to his old job, he joined the Wyant firm in 1948.

A big sandy-haired, blue-eyed man who seems much younger than his fifty-six years, Bristol looks more like a professor of engineering than someone who influences the investment of some $1.4 billion. Though Bristol's personal style tends toward self-effacement, he talks with feeling about schools and their investment problems: Those schools which allow banks to run their money "deserve better than that," he says. Many schools make their own investment decisions, he goes on. Without deprecating the dedication and the ability of trustees, he is concerned that those institutions that depend entirely on their trustees for counsel generally cannot move fast enough to take advantage of crucial investment opportunities. His own ability to get a quick reaction by phone from the investment committee members of his schools, he cites as vital in today's fast-moving financial world. "This is not a part-time business," he says. "These schools need the services of professional managers."

Bristol's school clients range in size from Princeton, with about $475 million, down to Seton Hall University, with about $4 million, and each has its own special problems and working conditions. The small colleges like Colby (a private college in Waterville, Maine) are squeezed between a need for money and the absence of affluent alumni to the degree of annual giving that Princeton, for instance, can take for granted.

The firm's work for Howard University, the Negro institution in Washington, D.C., a school with almost no endowment to start with, has been particularly gratifying to Bristol because the school's trustees have been extremely easy to work with, and have deferred consistently to his recommendations; and because he feels that Howard, more than most other schools, needs everything it can get. In 1951, the historical book value of the school's endowment stood at $1,427,000 and its market value at $1,661,000. Recently, when the book value was $5.5 million, market value was about $15 million.

The schools with large endowments have a different set of problems. A fund the size of Princeton's for practical reasons cannot have many small positions. Yet it is often hard to buy enough of a security to make a substantial investment, say $1 million or more. Princeton's portfolio contains, Bristol estimates, over two hundred different names. He shakes his head and his brow wrinkles: "Too many, we have many too many. I would say we've got a hundred fifty names of common stocks in here and I personally think we should have fifty." But even as large a number as a hundred fifty common stocks means that the average position in Princeton's $400 million portfolio is over $2 million.

Another persistent problem is that big gifts often come

in with strings attached. Bristol can speak with a kind of quiet exasperation about those gifts of securities that carry a stipulation prohibiting their sales. While schools have increased their efforts to persuade benefactors to give without strings attached, he still is helpless to deal with those strings already in place, which can be most frustrating when some stock bequeathed to be held in perpetuity becomes a prime candidate for sale. Another sort of string he mentions with concern is the one that limits the use of the gifts.

He cites a large bequest to Princeton that originally required that its earnings be devoted to scholarships for "poor boys from Jersey City," as the donor put it. The income would have been so large that it would have been difficult to find enough Jersey City candidates to use up the money. Just before he died, however, the donor at least agreed to extend its scope to high school graduates in all of New Jersey.

The investment tactic for which Bristol is most well-known is buying bonds that contain either "equity kickers" or options to buy common stock. And it is these deals which have brought him his most spectacular successes.

He outlines the philosophy: "This is what we always want: a present return and a stake in the future of the business. We want to earn something while we're waiting for the company to develop. My idea is to get income from the bond while getting the equity feature for nothing."

Since it's usually the companies not very well known in investment circles that give away equity with bonds, Bristol often must concentrate on small, newer companies. But this has worked out well for him. One of his most promising deals involves McDonald's, Inc., the highly successful system of franchised drive-in restaurants. His firm was approached in 1961 by McDonald's then-president, Harry J. Sonneborn, and board chairman Ray A. Krock, who wanted to borrow $2,700,000 in order to buy ninety-nine-year franchise rights from the two McDonald brothers. Bristol was interested, but insisted on getting stock in the company along with interest on the loans. Sonneborn and Krock, however, had no desire to dilute their equity in the company.

Another deal was then hammered out which nevertheless provided Bristol with a share in McDonald's future profits (the kicker) along with current yield. For the loan of $2,700,000, made jointly by a group of Bristol clients, they would receive 6 per cent interest on the unpaid balance. Meanwhile, they would receive ½ of 1 per cent of the new owners' gross until the debt was fully repaid. Then they would continue to receive that amount off the top for a period exactly equal to the time it took to pay back the principal.

The loan was fully repaid four years and eleven months after it was made, during which time the Bristol clients received their 6 per cent. But on the 1966 repayment date, the bonus period began, to continue for the contracted four years and eleven months. In 1967, thanks to the spectacular growth of McDonald, Bristol clients received around $1,500,-000 as their thin cut of the $300,000,000 pie. That means that the total return to the investors during this bonus period will probably amount to something in excess of $7,500,000. And, of course, the loan has been repaid—and at what was then a nice interest rate.

Another kicker Bristol likes is warrants. In 1957 Bristol purchased for clients $1 million in Coastal States Gas Producing Company bonds, paying 5½ per cent interest and carrying warrants to buy 180,000 shares at $2.50 per share. Before the warrants expired in June 1967, holders bought

180,000 shares of Coastal stock currently valued at about $45 on the NYSE.

Bristol also acquires a yield-plus-kicker by buying convertible debentures (bonds which can be converted into common stock at a stipulated price). Bristol cites an investment he made for clients back in 1955 in Litton. "I didn't see how we could go into an equity deal involving a stock with no early prospect of paying a cash dividend. But we did go in with convertible debentures." Princeton's original investment was $200,000 worth of 5 per cent convertible debentures. In 1962, another $239,000 was invested to exercise some rights. Against this investment of $439,000, a profit of about $305,000 was made through the subsequent sale of some of the shares, and the present market value of the Princeton Litton holding is about $11 million.

A look at the record of Princeton's bond holdings makes him smile at the departure from tradition and orthodoxy: "There's hardly a rated bond on this list. I mean we rate them, our way." His way: "We look at bonds the same way we look at stocks. Our rating is based on our faith in the industry and in the company, not on the mechanical means that Moody's and Standard and Poor's use. We aren't as scientific; our rating is more by the seat of our pants."

Bristol thinks colleges should not buy straight bonds. "The only excuse for being in them," he says, "is the need for current income." Bristol has occasionally bought them, but only when the money is so tight that handsome interest rates abound. Last summer, for instance, when straight bonds drew 6 to 6½ per cent, "We bought some ten to fifteen year things with sinking funds that would get us out of them pretty fast."

Bristol's stock purchases, like his yield-plus-kicker buys,

tend to be in small, promising companies. Most have paid off handsomely. The following, for example, were recently the largest equity holdings in Swarthmore's portfolio: $306,000 in Coastal States Gas has grown to $960,000; $90,000 of International Flavors & Fragrances is worth $3.1 million; Betz Laboratories, purchased three years ago for $314,000, has grown to $1.3 million. A man on the Street who has worked with colleges says of their willingness to accept this kind of investment, "When a trustee is second-guessing you all the time, you take the easy way out and bring in du Pont. You give those good ones to the people who listen to you."

Bristol finds private placements (letter stocks or bonds sold privately to institutions) particularly gratifying forms of investment for colleges, even when they are not so resoundingly successful as McDonald's and Coastal States. "We can usually come up with $2 to 3 million from among our clients, and we can tailor the deal to our particular needs."

These investments would of course be inappropriate for many clients, for the private placement locks the investor in. But Bristol, of course, does not need to sell in a hurry. Indeed, he prefers not to sell at all.

"We never sell a common stock unless we have lost confidence in the management or the industry," he says. "We might lighten up a little in some marginal situations if the market looks very vulnerable but we'll usually ride our stocks down rather than gamble on being able to buy back cheaper." Bristol does not believe in trying to catch short swings, since he buys on fundamentals and is looking for growth companies with good long-term prospects. "If you sell one of those companies," he says, "you have to be right twice because you're going to want to buy it back again."

He looks for steady, long term growth rather than cyclical growth, again because he does not want timing to be the most important factor in his buy-sell plans. Two other features he looks for in a company are inflation resistance and low labor costs.

If these policies have made returns to his clients pleasing, returns from the schools to the firm are quite unspectacular. Colleges simply do not pay as much as other kinds of institutional investors. Though universities account for far more than half of his business as far as assets managed goes, they account for far less than half his revenues.

Colleges sometimes argue, he says, "that they can't justify paying a person more than they pay their president." The real reason is usually that the trustees of endowment funds are often bankers who have done the job for nothing—albeit on a part-time basis—and they tend to think that everyone doing work of this sort for a college should do it for nothing or only a grudging little more.

Bristol stresses the importance of having a small investment committee at the university. If unanimous agreement is needed before a stock may be bought, a smaller group speeds up the decision-making time. He points to the unfortunate example of a professional investment man hampered by an investment committee of fifteen prominent citizens from the large city in which the university found itself—"all prima donnas, every one." Their wide variety of prejudices practically hamstrung the professional. Now he has managed to whittle his committee down to five.

Bristol has fared better. Princeton's investment committee, for instance, never numbers more than three.

Does he insist on a free hand in managing college money? "Of course I'd like to, but it is primarily the responsibility of the trustees. They must make the final decision. Our role is no different from a lawyer's or a doctor's. We tell the trustees what we think they should do. In the majority of cases they should go along with our advice or else find a new advisor."

Bristol says he is fortunate in having active and sophisticated investment committees. Princeton's chairman, Harvey Mole, is a full-time professional investor in his own right, being in charge of U.S. Steel's pension funds. Thomas B. McCabe, chairman of Scott Paper Co., guides Swarthmore's investment committee; before each meeting he takes his list of stocks, (he's not interested in bonds) pencils in the five-year earnings record, and calculates the compound growth rate. Then he'll challenge Bristol with some stock whose earnings "don't seem to be going anywhere. Why do we hold it?" Bristol likes this. It keeps him on his toes. "All of us need a hair shirt once in a while," he says.

Too, Bristol feels fortunate because his committees rarely try to influence his choice of brokers. Princeton, for one, gives him complete freedom; with so many Princeton men in Wall Street, attempts to do business with all of them would create infinite complications.

Bristol is certain that small colleges, needing to raise substantial funds for endowment, must convince alumni and potential donors that their funds will be intelligently handled. It follows that trustees will recognize the need for, and high value of, professional advice.

But the high administrative costs make it impractical for a professional to supervise small endowment funds on an individual basis. "It pains me to tell somebody that he's got too little money to manage individually," Bristol says, "but it costs me just as much to manage $250,000 as $2,500,000. And I worry much more."

Bristol thinks a good solution might be a mutual fund with a portfolio tailor-made for this class of investor. "But I'm afraid a major hurdle would be getting certain trustees to delegate responsibility to this extent."

When he's not at work in his office six blocks north of Wall Street, Bristol retreats as quickly as possible to his home in Great Swamp, New Jersey (near Morristown), where he lives with his wife and his two daughters and her four children by a previous marriage. His older daughter works for Vance Sanders and the younger is a student at the University of Pennsylvania. He recently contributed to a fund which bought 3700 acres of the Great Swamp and gave it to the Interior Department in hopes that this wildlife refuge would not be the victim of a proposed jetport. His tract (actually about a mile from the swamp), is "about four or five acres that I really enjoy puttering on. I love golf but I'm such a miserable player I cut the grass to run away from my game."

He speaks of golf in another context. "I want to tell you this business is like golf: It is a very 'umbling business. We've got some nice ones in here (he taps a computer print-out of his portfolios), but we've also got some that aren't so nice."

One that wasn't so nice: On his recommendation a number of his colleges combined to put over $1 million into the bonds of Wise Homes, Inc., a shell-home developer, a few years before the company went down in flames. Bristol says this experience was "traumatic" and that he heard angry words from alumni, though the trustees were generally more understanding. "One turkey," he says, "and you really get blasted."

Bristol stresses that this is an expected concomitant of the kind of policy that buys a Betz or a Coastal States. "Wise Homes looked just as good at the outset," Bristol insists. He practically tugs at the visitor's lapels to make his point, his

head tipped to one side and a typical smile-and-frown combination on his deeply lined face.

"If you're going to pursue an aggressive investment policy
you're going to have occasional losers. But some trustees [his,
he says, are an exception] and most alumni don't realize this.
The only stocks they notice are Wise Homes and Atlantic
Acceptance [another losing stock some of Bristol's clients
were in]. They forget about the Xeroxes.

"It's all very well to be orthodox and to shuffle through
triple-A bonds and such. But the true test of being conservative is being right in the future." And with college expenses
growing far faster than endowments and tuition, being right
in the future, he feels, requires aggressive investing.

ROLAND GRIMM
The university
as a fund manager

OLAND D. GRIMM is president of Endowment Management & Research, and is responsible, to a significant degree, for bringing the advantages of performance to the university. However he doesn't talk much about which stocks are going up or why. You may sit down to find out which groups are hot, and find yourself learning something about palm reading instead.

"I started to do palm reading when I was studying psychology," he notes. "I believe all these things like graphology and phrenology can tell us something about what's going on inside people." Grimm opens his own palm. His hands are large, and the fingers broad and blunt. The primary lines in the palm, those of head, heart, and life, are deep and unbroken. They look like highways, not split and winding trails the way they do on most people. According to Grimm this indicates an open and rather single-minded person. A person with one set of goals and one unconflicting set of emotions.

In a sense this is misleading. Grimm's goals and emotions may be clear and unidirectional, but his interests are not. Before turning to the stock market, he got a master's degree in psychology. He collects, and at one time had a business in, antiques. He enjoys gardening, and has bought a commercial greenhouse which he is converting into a combination indoor swimming pool and noncommercial greenhouse. He dug the pool himself; it took him and a caretaker several spring weekends.

Grimm hardly comes on the way this outdoor activity and those large, blunt-fingered hands might imply. Tall, quiet and urbane, he gives an impression of innate elegance, eminently suited to his role as president of the company that manages Yale University's half billion. Thinly rimmed tortoise-shell glasses perch at an angle on his large, round face. The face is often laughing; Roland Grimm is a happy man, not a brooder. "My philosophy of life is enjoy," he says, "you only come this way once."

This man occupies a unique position in the investment community today. He is president of an investment counseling firm half-owned by a university. And half the money this firm invests belongs to that university: it consists of the more than $500 million of Yale University's endowment fund.

Grimm's association with a staid university is an excellent example of the change that has come over universities' attitudes toward their endowment funds; for he is a model of the new generation of aggressive, performance-minded money managers.

For Grimm, it all began one day in March 1967. Grimm, then vice-president of Fidelity Management & Research, and manager of its Fidelity Fund and Contra Fund, was on vacation in Spain, looking at cathedrals and sleeping in the sun. The trans-Atlantic telephone call which interrupted his vacation was from Yale, his alma mater. Yale wanted help in replanning the investment operation of its $500 million endowment. By the time he headed back, Grimm had some definite feelings and ideas.

What sent Yale to the telephones was a kind of financial crisis. With an annual outgo of close to $100 million, the university was spending more than its income annually. While the Yale endowment was performing no worse than that of comparable institutions, it wasn't increasing fast enough to absorb this kind of spending, much less what would be required for the needs Yale could foresee.

When the negotiations were all over, a new firm emerged on the investment scene: Endowment Management & Research. Yale owned half. The other half was owned by three Boston managers associated with performance funds— Grimm, Frank Ingraham from Keystone S-4, and Joseph McNay of the Massachusetts Company. Yale's new financial helmsmen were, respectively, forty-two, thirty-three and thirty-two.

Yale's president, Kingman Brewster, Jr., considered New York for the site of the new firm, but only briefly. There were so many Yale alumni on the Street that relationships might have become a little tangled. Boston, of course, was the Camp of the Other Guys, but "I have my own untutored, unprofessional reasons for wanting it there. They might as well put up two thermometers on the Boston Common," says Kingman Brewster, referring to the rivalry. Ultimately it was because the finalists in Yale's management derby—Bostonians all—wanted to stay there that Endowment Management settled there. "I told them," says Roland Grimm, "that Boston was the finest financial center in the country. Those people in New York see only black and white; when they're bullish, they're totally bullish; when they're bearish, they're on the window sills. This is a better place for perspective."

At first, Yale asked Grimm to manage its endowment on a fee basis. "But I said 'no thank you, I'm not interested,'" says Grimm. "The only way to attract people who are on the inside track today is equity."

The arrangement that finally was settled on seems ideal for both parties. Grimm and his partners have a most unusual franchise—a half-billion-dollar endowment to manage. In turn, Yale has purchased the talents of three top money managers.

And it has purchased them cheap.

Although nobody is saying what the fee is for managing Yale's money, Grimm does mention that "it is in six figures." If it is $999,999, it is still less than one-fifth of one per cent of Yale's $540 million. And the better the endowment performs, the lower the fee in percentage terms, since it is a flat dollar sum. It is based not on the quality of the managers but on the costs of managing the half-billion dollars.

In addition, Yale gets the managers' most focused attention. "By setting up our own group," says president Brewster, "we had no legal or ethical problem with giving ourselves top priority. Other clients will know that we share on a priority basis any good ideas that the firm generates."

Other clients have been chosen so as to enhance the management of the Yale money. At present, the bulk of them are other charitable institutions. The second largest group is corporate pension and profit-sharing plans. Grimm expects the latter ultimately to become bigger than the former "because one group is stagnant and the other is growing very fast." EM&R also has several individual accounts (minimum accepted: $1 million). All these clients are chosen for their involvement in many political and economic arenas, making them good sources of information.

In the same pursuit of keeping informed, Grimm sits on the boards of many institutions, and spends a good deal of time on the road to and from meetings. He won't say just how many boards "because somebody might think I don't have any time left for my job," he says. But actually, he considers that this work makes him better able to perform his job: "There's no doubt but that we're in a tremendous state of flux and it's terribly important to develop a feel for which way things are moving. You certainly can't do that by being holed up somewhere."

Grimm has developed some very definite ideas of where things are moving in the investment world at the moment. He has ideas about what sorts of companies will perform well and what sorts will not, about changes taking place in the habits of big investors and Wall Street brokers, and about which investors are going to do well over the next few years. They are not the kind of ideas one used to hear voiced in the immediate vicinity of university money. "Listen," he says with emphasis, "the whole investment business is changing. It's going to make *investors* out of people, long-term investors.

"The problem really revolves around the fact that there is more money seeking performance than there are stocks that can provide it. Overall, people can only get average results.

"Performance is going to get much harder to come by. For one thing, some performance lately has been manufactured because of what companies have been able to do in the merger area. The present [Nixon] Administration is changing

the rules so as to fix that. Another source of outstanding performance that has been removed is inside information."

The most profound changes that are making performance
difficult, perhaps, are the changes in what brokerage houses
are offering their clients.

"In the old days," Grimm continues, "people like myself
could just sit around and get visits from Wall Street analysts.
Each would produce one idea—one good idea—a year, but
that was enough. Anybody could make money.

"This has changed. The problem, and for a long time I
didn't see it, is that the commodity everybody was buying
with his commission dollars isn't the same thing as it was as
recently as three years ago. In addition, because of the enormous speculative bull market of the last two years, the quality of research work being done recently has been very poor.
The trouble was that people could make money with any
investment. If a company wasn't a good thing in itself then
it had value as a takeover candidate.

"Also, we're simply not getting the best ideas these firms
generate early enough any more. The reason is simple: they're
going into their customers' businesses: investment counseling, mutual fund management, etc. So now when you get
an idea it's got to be skim milk; it's got to be inflated by their
having recommended it first to their advisory clients. When
you've got a counseling business are you going to trot up to
Roland Grimm and give him your best ideas? You've got to
be crazy!

"The net of this as I see it is that, as I mentioned, people
are going to become investors instead of traders. Investment
managers are going to have to make up their minds about a
company and stick with it. Since everybody is getting into
everybody else's business, this means that companies are

going to have to do their own research work, requiring larger and larger staffs.

"Consequently the pendulum is swinging back from the multiple manager concept which is currently all the rage, back to the analyst. What's going to be important is having facts. What's going to be important is making judgments about what will happen two years from now, not what will happen tomorrow."

This is one factor that will influence what stocks will do well over the next few years. Another, in Grimm's view, is a revolution that is taking place in the habits of some of the largest institutional investors.

"We're in the process of converting savings from fixed dollars to variable dollars, from bonds to equities. Insurance companies are acquiring mutual funds to give them equity expertise. Pension funds are moving increasingly into common stocks.

"You can divide the sources of this new demand for equities into two groups: the big money—everything upwards of $500 million—and the rest. I think it's perfectly clear that there's more big money than anything else.

"The most logical area of investment for these institutions is investment-grade securities, major companies like U. S. Steel. For one thing, these are the closest in spirit to the bonds they've been holding.

"There is another reason too. As they look for equities they can either get a real laundry list—lots of small holdings—or they can acquire big positions in a few companies. I think they'll do the latter because they won't have the manpower to analyze a laundry list."

Factors internal to the companies themselves and in the economy in general will also tend to push the value of the majors up, Grimm believes. "I think we're going to see a very real rise in earning power in the basic industries in the next few years," he says. "Demand is rising as the population grows, yet in many industries presently slack times or tight money are keeping them from adding capacity. What will happen is what happened in the lumber industry, where the prices of materials and end products doubled because demand rose but capacity didn't.

"The companies that will do well in the next two years fall into three groups. First, the pot of gold companies. The companies where there is going to be a boom and everybody knows it. Nobody discounts this kind of future growth enough. Thus, Walt Disney with its resort building is a good buy. Kaiser Steel is a good buy because of its iron ore subsidiary in Australia, Hammersley Iron. Also Atlantic Richfield.

"The advantage of this type of security is that when it goes down it doesn't go down very far. (Unless, of course, the price is based on a myth and that myth is exploded.) Take for instance Caterpillar in the 50's. Or Polaroid now: it suffers by near-term costs but if you're sufficiently far-sighted (most investors aren't) it will pay off big.

"A second group of stocks that will do well are the recovery candidates, the ones that have a business that's presently running on 4 of its 6 cylinders. An example of this is the agricultural chemicals business of W. R. Grace. If you think agricultural chemicals will come back this is a great stock, because right now nobody's making much money in this area so they're not building any more capacity.

"Another example of this second group is Clorox. This stock is out of favor now because everybody else is putting enzymes into their products. But *Consumer Reports* says the enzymes don't do any good. So if people come back to Clorox, which is a recognized bleach and disinfectant, it will do very well.

"A third group of stocks that are good is the demography stocks; that is crystal clear. The stocks that benefit from the age distribution of the population. For instance there are more and more people in the twenty-five to thirty-five age bracket. Presumably this will, for the time at least, mean more and more marriages. So just to begin with everybody's going to need a bed. Simmons should do well. They'll also need a refrigerator and a stove and a hi-fi.

"There are more and more old people too. But I think the nursing homes craze has been pretty well overdone."

What won't do well over the next two years? "I think the conglomerates are pretty dead for a while. One reason is internal to the companies: their chief officers are going to have to change from being stock market operators to being business managers. They won't all make it."

In sum, Grimm says, "I would say you've got a two-year bull market in the major industrial corporations coming. This situation ought to have run its course by 1972. The big corporations will have had their big growth and they'll go to sleep again.

"But in the meantime I think we'll see large money making substantial gains if it can get out of the bonds it's now stuck with and into equities of the same grade."

Probably as much as anything else, the personality and plans of EM&R's tall, forty-three year-old president will shape the future of the firm. Although Grimm is a native of New Paltz, New York, he has firm roots in Boston: his wife is the former Lucy Lowell, a member of the family that talks to the Cabots while the Cabots are talking to God, in the old poem about Boston snobbishness. Despite his strong ties with a very Harvard family, Grimm went to Yale in 1946, after two years in the Army; he graduated in 1950. From there he went, not to Wall Street, but farther uptown to Teacher's College at Columbia University, where he earned his master's degree in social psychology.

His interest in psychology jibes well with his approach to the market. He believes human nature is the major determinant that does not change.

He says he left the social psychology field because "I was very discouraged; it seemed to me that in order to make a mark you had to rewrite the textbook that the last guy who got his master's had rewritten." So after receiving his master's degree in 1951, he went to work as a trainee at the First National Bank in Boston, where he wandered through various departments before settling into research work in the First's trust department, the Old Colony Trust Company. Why did he switch from psychology to banking? "To tell the truth, it was the only job I could find."

The Old Colony started him at $2000 a year. When he got married a year later, he and his wife survived by living over her parents' garage. (Presumably they were also getting asked to dinner in the main house.) In 1954, when Grimm left Old Colony, he was earning $4500. "They were thinking of paying me $12,000 when I matured and this and that," he recalls. "Of course they've revised their salary scale somewhat since then." From '54 to '56 he did research and trading at the Massachusetts Hospital Life Insurance Company. After a subsequent five years doing research at Massachusetts Investors Trust, he went in 1961 to his last position before starting EM&R: portfolio manager of the Fidelity Fund, Inc. (From late 1966, when it started, he managed

Fidelity's new Contra Fund as well.) Finally, in October, 1967, he settled down in a bright corner room which overlooks the cranes and derricks that are building the New Boston, and the golden dome of the State House and steeple of the Old North Church that are symbols of the Old. Its walls and those of the surrounding corridors are covered with old prints, oils, and watercolors of pre-twentieth-century ships in full sail. They came from his home in suburban Westwood, where he lives with his wife and their three children. Three official documents on the wall, and the Paraguayan flag in front of his fireplace, attest to another position he holds. Since 1965, he has been the consul in Boston for Paraguay; friends in that country suggested him for the post. He says it is an entreé to many of the most interesting people he knows—those in the diplomatic community of Boston.

His reputation suggests that he is eminently well suited to a position requiring diplomacy. "Roly is the Number One gentleman in this business," says an admirer, voicing sentiments typical of the brokerage committee with which Grimm deals.

There is an air of exhilaration about EM&R. Grimm's excitement comes, he says, from the chance "to do for a university—perhaps for many universities—what has been done for the public for years through mutual funds, and to build a substantial capital asset for the people who work here." EM&R partner Ingraham says, less delicately but no less to the point, "It's a chance to make a social contribution and a lot of money."

Skeptics are critical of all this Higher Purpose, and the three men who founded EM&R admit that having Yale's money to manage is like having "a franchise to mine the lands belonging to the Hudson's Bay Company," as one of them puts it. Still they insist that making money for the university is one of the greatest potential satisfactions in this job.

After all, all had been successful portfolio managers before they started EM&R and all had made or inherited a good deal of money. Under these circumstances, Grimm says, "You can retire to the sidelines and enjoy life or you can make a contribution. If you've been given some talents and have done well for yourself with them I think you ought to give some of it back.

"The song says for God, for country and for Yale, doesn't it?" says Grimm. "I hope we can do well for Yale, and there's nothing more important for this country than the quality of her education. As for God, well I hope he is on our side."

VERNON EAGLE
The flight of a rare bird
in foundationland

"APPALLING!" The word shoots out of the side of his mouth at a high velocity, a sort of adjectival final volley in a particularly boisterous fusillade. Vernon A. Eagle, executive director of The New World Foundation, a small, $19 million organization dedicated to a variety of liberal, social and educational causes, draws deeply on his cigar, then—with a smile—slumps back in his chair.

He is especially pleased because he has just used one of his favorite words in discussing one of his favorite subjects: the antediluvian management of most foundation portfolios.

Those who have despaired that the go-go craze has swept away the venerable investment verities of high yield and preservation of capital may take solace. The Widows and Orphans are alive and well among the $20 billion in foundationland. The performance syndrome, which has created a

maelstrom even in such insulated havens as university endowment funds and union pension funds, has produced only the
most gossamer of ruffles at the foundations. Indeed, it is safe
to say that of all forms of institutional money, foundation
funds are managed with just about the most resolute, un-
swerving dedication to the traditions of yesteryear.

Foundationland is a strange, faraway world. In quiet
offices in the corners of lofty buildings, distinguished bankers,
noted educators, world-famous scientists and renowned hu-
manitarians make monthly musings over their foundation's
portfolio, to safeguard against the rude possibility that something that isn't "our kind of security." has slipped in. Such
off-color terms as "growth" and "capital appreciation" are
not heard—they do not square with "the way we've always
handled our funds." The abiding philosophy is to avoid taxes,
preserve the founder's good name and his stock holdings,
maintain the status quo and avoid personal embarrassment
and public criticism, especially wrath from Texas Congress-
man Wright Patman, who for the past seven years has been
conducting a vituperative crusade against private foundations.

A veil of deep secrecy is thus maintained. Many foundations issue no annual reports or public statements of any
kind. Questions from outsiders are often regarded as potential threats, and comment is refused until lawyers are consulted.

It is all a somewhat paradoxical spectacle. Foundations
built on the fortunes of ruthlessly capitalistic entrepreneurs
now turn away in horror from the slightest investment risk.
Foundations that make zealous efforts to contribute to the
betterment of man seem not to have the slightest interest
in the betterment of their yield. Instead, they have devised

an abundantly top-heavy system of committees, policies, and procedures that, good markets and bad, keeps often 40 per cent or more of their assets locked in fixed-income securities, ensuring annual spendable yields (including capital gains) of under 4 per cent.

Cautious management ranges from the big to the small. Everyone's exhibit A is the Ford Foundation, by far the largest foundation, with close to $4 billion in assets. Ford president McGeorge Bundy saw fit in 1966 to excoriate college and university endowment fund trustees for their lackadaisical investment policies: "Over the long run, caution has cost our colleges and universities much more than imprudence or excessive risk taking." Yet his own foundation, it is widely pointed out, continues to keep a billion dollars stuffed away in bonds and notes. According to a 1966 *Fortune* study, Ford's portfolio lagged far behind the Dow Jones Average between 1956 and 1966.

Then there is the portfolio of a small ($27 million) research-oriented organization. It recently included nearly $10 million in cash or fixed-income securities and the rest in a group of common stocks that could well be a computer read-out of issues least likely to increase in price over the next ten years.

Responsible for this less than adventurous line-up was the chairman of the Finance Committee, a man in his late seventies. According to friends, he was convinced that a great financial panic is almost upon us, and he was determined not to be trampled in the race to the exit.

It is the ideas of foundation men like this that Vernon Eagle is vigorously trying to combat. Eagle is indeed a *rara avis*—or, in his words, a "lifelong activist." He is short, rather heavy, with black, slightly askew hair. He appears, at forty-nine, to be at some indescribable halfway-point between an SDS militant and a musty curmudgeon. His eyes dance with an incendiary gleam while his body is enveloped in a somber, dark financial uniform.

"The attitude of most foundation trustees is in the grand Lady Bountiful tradition, in other words, just plain stupid," he goes on, warming to the subject on which he will discourse at length with anyone. "They just don't seem to realize that the more money you can make, the more things you can do. The problem is that most of them know nothing about finance, and they simply don't want to bother paying any attention to their portfolios. So what you get is the finance committee of the foundation working with the finance committee of a bank—which almost ensures getting the lowest common denominator of both. Investment by committee does not usually yield very imaginative results. And look at the Carnegie Corporation. Have you ever noticed their performance? I mean you really have to work hard to do that badly."

Lambasting foundation management has become, he says, "something of a crusade for me." Recently he addressed a symposium at the National Council on Foundations in Kansas City. Probably expecting a droning dirge of dusty erudition on the relative merits of AAA vs. AA bonds, the members of the audience were rudely startled when Eagle commenced a typically full-bore blast.

"I told them that they were trying to hide behind their fiduciary role—the Prudent Man and that sort of thing," Eagle says. "I remarked that what they were doing was neither prudent nor even conservative. They were not conserving. Their money was actually losing its value. I said they had to take some risks and that if they didn't make a few mistakes, they weren't doing their jobs. They thought I was a heretic. They looked at me as if they simply could not believe any board could let such a man run its money."

Eagle's portfolio at The New World Foundation is not exactly run like a hedge fund, of course. He has had to confront many of the same problems facing investment managers in other foundations: initially a one-stock grant and a less than financially aggressive board headed by a relative of the donor. The foundation was begun in 1954 with a block of shares in International Harvester from the estate of Anita McCormick Blaine, daughter of Cyrus McCormick. Anne Blaine Harrison, wife of *The New Republic* publisher Gilbert Harrison, executor of her grandmother's will, and president of the New World board, is anything but the traditional, party-giving heiress. "She is a staunch liberal," says Eagle. "She's done things like help work as an organizer for the textile workers down in South Carolina during the 1940's."

Mrs. Harrison and the rest of the board gave Eagle full responsibility for selecting investments, and made no objections when he promptly unloaded the International Harvester. "It just wasn't a good investment for us," he says. They also went along with Eagle's desire to switch advisors from a bank in Chicago which was managing some of Mrs. Harrison's money, and with which some of the New World trustees had close ties, to the fairly aggressive Wall Street counseling firm of John W. Bristol & Co. (see p. 177), which specializes in the management of nonprofit institutional accounts. The board does dictate the general policy, though, and it ruled that the proceeds from the sale of the Harvester stock be divided equally between stocks and bonds.

Even with these restrictions, the New World portfolio has achieved impressive results. As we have seen, Bristol is known

for his ability to secure high-coupon private placement bonds
with provision for conversion to common stock, and the New
World's fixed-income issues yield over 6.5 per cent. The
stocks, meanwhile, have nearly quadrupled. Bristol and Eagle
tend toward smaller growth companies that enable one to
participate, as Eagle says, "in the possible expansion explosion
that occasionally does take place in some of the smaller companies." They bought, for example, Coastal States Gas at 4,
International Flavors and Fragrances at 5, Russell Stover at
5, Transamerica at 16, and Famous Artists Schools at 3. All
have since appreciated over 300 per cent,—some as high as
1000 per cent.

Eagle currently takes a "cautiously optimistic" view of
the market, though he is always worried about the possible
effects of the war in Vietnam. He notes that he is "shying
away from the high fliers which I think are badly overpriced," and sticking with special situations and private
placements. "The speculative fever worries me," he says.

"If I had my own way completely, I'd be all in stocks,"
he says. "But it is the board's responsibility to set policy
according to its best judgment." Spending capital gains is
permitted, though not a regular practice, and Eagle feels that
as the assets increase in size the foundation will tend more
toward the "total return" concept of not distinguishing between yield and capital gains. The idea is that return is
return, and where it should come from depends on the realities of the stock market, not on a preconceived judgment of
how much money should be in bonds compared to stocks.

This refusal to casually accept the status quo is not surprising, considering Eagle's background. He was born in the
tiny farming village of Britt, Iowa, the next to youngest of

six children. When he was three, his mother and father broke up, leaving the children in various foster homes and orphanages. Eagle has not seen his father since.

His childhood, he remembers, was a very emotionally upsetting experience. "I'm not sure I should be telling you all this," he says. "I wasn't able to talk about it with anyone until I went through analysis. I know most of my friends will be shocked to hear about it. They've always considered me an old-line Ivy Leaguer."

When he was seven, he began working as a "hired hand" on the farm of the family with whom he was staying. "I didn't think so at the time," he says, "but it was the best possible training anyone could have. You learned to cope. If some machinery broke down, you learned how to fashion a new part." His formal education was erratic. Finally he began attending a Catholic seminary, the Society of the Divine Word, for boys studying for the priesthood. It was by far, he says, the best free education around. "It was truly classical, just as good as Andover or Exeter with plenty of Latin and Greek." But he had great difficulty stomaching the religious accoutrements, and, after four years, just before he was due to receive the equivalent of a high school diploma, he was expelled.

"I had to put up or shut up." Eagle finally did get a diploma from a nearby high school, and went off to the University of Southern California. But in the meantime, like many Americans in the 1930's, he had become deeply involved with the Spanish Civil War. "I was really turned on," he remembers. "It was like Vietnam is for the kids today." When Hitler began marching through Europe, he was terribly frustrated by the unconcern among the other students at USC: "They just didn't seem to care." He decided, "I had to do something. I had to put up or shut up." He quit school in 1939 and joined up with the British commandos.

It was an exciting, "all-consuming" experience. The commandos were divided into small guerrilla units, composed of very young, idealistic men who constantly operated behind enemy lines. But in 1943, in North Africa, Eagle was badly wounded. He spent the next eight months in various hospitals, and his leg had to be amputated. While convalescing in a Staten Island hospital, he met John K. Oliphant, then executive vice-president for the Central Hanover Bank, who urged him to come into banking. "I didn't have anything else to do," says Eagle, "and he told me that a background in banking would be useful in whatever I ended up doing later on."

After a couple of years in a training program, and some night courses in economics, law, and international finance at NYU and Columbia, he was sent to London to work in the bank's international division, which he later headed. He found the experience much more interesting than domestic banking. "It wasn't so parochial and dull," he recalls. "If you met with a banker in Munich, sure you discussed banking. But you probably also talked about art, literature, and philosophy. If he were entertaining you, you'd go to the opera, not a musical comedy."

Eagle's real passion, though, continued to be several liberal causes back home. He and a number of friends, such as cartoonist Bill Mauldin, Gilbert Harrison, Gus Tyler of the ILGWU, lawyer Orin Root, Adam Yarmolinsky, former Deputy Assistant Secretary of Defense, and Charles Bolte, vice-president of the Carnegie Endowment for International

Peace, established the American Veterans Committee, which announced itself as for just about everything the American Legion was against. Its motto was: "Americans first, veterans second." Despite its small size, the AVC, which included several journalists and writers, made a loud noise and did much to combat the national postwar slide into isolationism. It championed such causes as the United Nations and foreign aid. "The trouble with the AVC," an American legionnaire remarked at the time, "is that every one of its members owns a typewriter."

Another of Eagle's friends at the AVC was a young Sarah Lawrence student named Ann Sickels, whom he later married. They now have two daughters and one son—two in college and the youngest in private school—and live in a rural section of Rockland County.

When Gilbert Harrison's wife suggested that Eagle might come back to the United States to help organize The New World Foundation, he jumped at the opportunity. "I knew nothing about foundations," he says. "I had never even met a foundation executive. But I talked to several friends at the Fund for the Republic which the Ford Foundation had started—it was the peak of the Robert M. Hutchins era—and they seemed to be having a ball."

Though New World does not have the ample resources of many larger foundations, it has had a significant effect on those organizations on which it has chosen to concentrate. Eagle, who runs the grant program, has had the foundation give several hundred thousand dollars, for instance, to the Southern Regional Council, which has been actively engaged in combating racism, fostering voter education projects and working for school desegregation.

Whether Eagle will be as effective in his crusade for better foundation money management remains to be seen. "I wasn't terribly popular out there in Kansas City," he says. "But maybe what I said will start them thinking just a little bit. Maybe they'll go back to their offices and begin to ask a question or two."

THE SELF-STYLISTS 4

Introduction

THE MEN IN THIS FINAL SECTION are part of the age of performance, but they are just a little out of step with the others. They are happily following their own paths and, perhaps, pointing out the direction of the future. *Ed Merkle's* belief, for instance, is that your fund need not be at the top of the performance heap if you know how to employ the latest McLuhanistic media techniques to woo investors. Appropriately, Merkle's fund is called the Madison Fund and is located on Madison Avenue.

George Chestnutt is located even farther away from Wall Street: Greenwich, Conn. He makes a point of staying away from New York altogether. "Hate the place, always have, big, dirty place," he says. Chestnutt's special god is the Chart, a statistical concoction of mathematical ratios and multicolored graph lines which, he is certain, yield basic secrets about which stocks are about to move. *Bill O'Neil* is convinced the same secrets can be produced by his beloved IBM 360-40 computer, and he is sure that computer analysis of the market will be the wave of the future. O'Neil is located in Los Angeles, where all waves of the future begin to roll.

But suppose we should all grow weary of the stress and anxiety of constant striving for performance? Perhaps, as 'Adam Smith' suggests in his introduction, the Age of Performance will fade away to a new age and a new generation. A philosophy for calmer, quieter times could well be that of *Peter Bernstein,* noted lecturer, economist and rabbit-lover as well as investment counselor. He feels that the modern age is missing something, that holding one's client's hand is sometimes more important than putting him in the latest high flyers. "We feel our clients are people, not money," he says. "They are coming here to look for peace of mind. The name of the game is their happiness."

PETER BERNSTEIN
The art of
holding hands

P ETER BERNSTEIN likes managing people more than
he likes managing money.
 Though this is only one of a number of anomalous
things that can be said about Bernstein, noted economist
and investment counselor, it is the most important. One
might expect that a predilection for something other than
the basic manna of Wall Street could be debilitating, if
not fatal; however Bernstein is proof that the successful
management of money need not entail misanthropy or a ruth-
less striving for performance.

He looks at money, for example, almost completely in
human terms. "I feel that money should be spent or used,"
he says. "It represents the opportunity to achieve power, to
do good works or bad works. But it should not just be accumulated." He feels that too many people worship money

for its own sake to the exclusion of other concerns. "The problem with this country," he says, "is that we don't care about other people. We neglect other people's problems if they don't happen to be our problems. And in our ambition to get ahead we don't care if we step on somebody else to do it."

Bernstein wears horn-rimmed glasses and a carefully groomed moustache. He is always amused, not in the cynical French way but in the Central European way that finds delight in the incongruity of man's position of power on a planet large enough to ignore him completely. His iconoclasm, his delight in twitting the sensibilities of others, though, is tempered with easy graciousness. He fits in comfortably among the tasteful English antiques and ornate red-leather desk in his Wall Street office, an office whose door is almost always open.

One is not surprised to learn that he and his wife own a cat named Sidney and two pet rabbits named Dominica and Angelique. (His first rabbit, Prospero, who was named after *The Price of Prosperity*, Bernstein's first book, died in 1963.) One is not surprised either that once, in the middle of a very important business lunch, he abruptly excused himself to call his veterinarian and check on one of his rabbits who was seriously ill.

"Peter must be one of the world's best-liked human beings," says his long-time friend and fellow economist Robert L. Heilbroner. "He has an undisguised, uncontrived enjoyment of others, which brings its return measure. He has a real common touch, a complete absence of front. There is no barrier between him and other people."

Peter Bernstein is chairman of Bernstein-Macaulay, an investment counseling firm which recently merged with the

New York Stock Exchange member house of Cogan, Berlind, Weill and Levitt to become that firm's investment management subsidiary. Under Bernstein's aegis are over four hundred accounts with some $500 million in assets, only about 20 per cent of which involve holdings of $1 million or more.

Bernstein does not agree with the prevailing view on Wall Street that the maximum possible physical distance must be maintained between counsel and client; that the client's presence is about as useful and desirable as that of a throng of spectators during a heart transplant operation.

"We feel our clients are people, not money," he says, "and the name of the game is their happiness. They are coming here to look for peace of mind. Of course some clients think we're heros even when we're not doing particularly well for them in handling their portfolio, while others are unhappy even if we're doing far better than anyone could reasonably expect. In either case we believe that hand-holding is a vital part of this business."

In setting up an account, he goes on, "we try to determine the amount of money a person can or should risk in order to achieve his desired objective, whether it is simply to obtain income for the preservation of capital or to achieve capital growth. In making this determination we have to take into account all of a man's life forces: his family relationships, his job, whether he is happily married, the age and status of his children and his aspirations for the future. We try to see him in the whole."

When a strategy is worked out, either Bernstein (who personally handles a large number of accounts) or one of the other officers contacts the client at least once a month either by letter, telephone or over lunch, to discuss the status of the portfolio. Each account meanwhile is reviewed twice a month, once by the account executive and another time by one of the firm's other members.

While Bernstein does believe in plenty of client contact, he admits that he wishes his firm had greater discretionary power over many of the accounts—Bernstein-Macaulay has complete freedom to act in somewhat less than half the accounts. "An investment advisor simply does better when he can work on a discretionary basis," he maintains. "He can be more decisive and he doesn't have to spend a lot of time and energy bringing the client around to his point of view. I'm afraid that when the account is nondiscretionary, the client is simply getting the best of your salesmanship and not the best of your judgment."

A distinctive characteristic of Peter Bernstein is his dual role as an investment manager and an economist. Writing about economics is his abiding avocation. Whether at his apartment on Manhattan's East Side or his rural retreat in New England, he arises promptly at six o'clock and then, dressed in bathrobe and slippers, spends an hour and a half at the typewriter before heading for the office. ("Peter has none of the blockages to work that other people seem to have," says Heilbroner. "Maybe it would be a little better if it were not so easy for him.")

Bernstein readily jokes about his writing: "Clients tend to think you're something of a celebrity when you write books, and that doesn't hurt business." This conclusion isn't held by everyone, though. He tells the story of the wife of a potential client who interviewed him at his office. "When I showed her some of my books," he remembers, "she said she wanted to know when I had time to watch the market. Then she stomped out of the office." He still takes his writing quite seriously, though. "Money aside, I would rather be an economist," he says. "I would love just to sit and write."

Bernstein's writing, though not exactly eloquent, is nonetheless lucid and straightforward. He is the author of two books: *The Price of Prosperity*, 1962, and *A Primer on Money, Banking and Gold*, 1965 (revised in 1968). He has done a number of magazine articles for such publications as *The Harvard Business Review, The New York Times Magazine* and professional economic journals. His monthly financial letter is read widely by economists as well as by several thousand institutional investors. He has supervised the editing of a series of economic primers for Random House. And just to be sure he doesn't have a lot of spare time on his hands, he has for some years taught night courses in monetary theory at the New School for Social Research.

Bernstein feels that his experience as an economist gives him an edge over other investment counselors in managing his clients' money. "I use economics in my thinking every day," he asserts. "It helps me to understand the capital market and its effect on business. It helps me to see the competitive forces at work in the marketplace, the ability of a firm to set its own prices." Adds one Wall Streeter, "Bernstein's ability to detect changes in the GNP, corporate profits and interest rates has often put him one up on other investment counselors."

His experience in economics has given him a special interest in fixed-income securities because the flow of the economy is so sharply reflected in the bond market. Too many investors and investment managers, he feels, shy away from bonds because they treat them simply as permanent investments. Yet by playing the yield curve and interest rate trends, he points out, you can make bonds a flexible investment vehicle that can and should produce trading profit just like stocks— and offer an interest return to boot. During periods of high interest rates last year, Bernstein repeatedly pointed out both to his individual and his institutional accounts the strong case that can be made for bonds. While long-term rates can be expected to remain at lofty levels, he wrote, a moderate decline was not inconceivable, and such a development would reward bond holders with a rise in market prices. Many of his accounts have accumulated profits by buying bonds during high rates and selling on the many downswings.

This approach raised eyebrows at many investment counseling firms where the typical approach, on receiving new business, is to sell quickly anything that isn't common stocks. When Bernstein-Macaulay was awarded the advisory contract for a union-management pension fund with assets of more than $20 million, 65 per cent of which was in bonds, ". . . we examined the portfolio carefully," says Bernstein, "but when we offered no reason for tampering with the bond account I think everyone was greatly surprised. The point was that the high yield on the bonds much more than covered the actuarial requirement, thus giving us an opportunity to be really aggressive with the common stocks."

In 1969, Bernstein's enthusiasm for bonds waned somewhat, and he switched a substantial amount of his bond money into AT&T, which he considered the equivalent of "an aggressive bond purchase. If bonds do well, AT&T will do better."

Bernstein's other investment philosophies are somewhat less unconventional. He believes strongly in concentrating on a minimum number of stocks. "Stocks can't go down more than 100 per cent but they can go up an infinite amount," he says. "That means if you give your winners a chance, they have to outweigh your losers. From this it follows that too much portfolio diversification is downright silly." Bernstein-Macaulay normally maintains a "buy" list of no more than twelve items. (Issues that have long been favored include IBM, Georgia Pacific and American Hospital Supply.) No new name is added until it is determined that an existing stock should be dropped. For the future, Bernstein sees maximum profit potential in the fields of education and construction. "Just look around you," he says. "Look at all those cities and all those people." He has recently bought Uris Buildings Corp. because "it has the right charisma for our time."

Bernstein's books, however, range far beyond investment philosophies and analyses of the economy, reflecting his central concern with people. Indeed the views he espouses are often at great variance with those of the wide majority of his more conservative colleagues. He has often supported and worked for such Democrats as Eugene McCarthy and has actively supported peace and anti-Vietnam organizations. He is strongly in favor, for example, of government spending and closing tax loopholes. Traditional conservative abhorrence of federal expenditures, he maintains, derives from what economist John Kenneth Galbraith has called "The evil reputation of bad kings." Spending, it was presumed, was for "the enrichment or enjoyment of the rulers rather than the improvement of the community." In reality, Bernstein argues, government spending today both increases the wealth of the private sector and provides income for people who otherwise wouldn't have any; such spending "must be seen as part of the dynamic process of economic growth."

The only kind of spending supported by conservatives, he points out, is for national defense which "epitomizes the maintenance of the status quo." Bernstein, further, strongly favors some government management of the economy, and in 1962 he and Heilbroner collaborated on a book specifically designed to aid the Kennedy Administration by explaining to the public the reasons behind the proposed tax cut.

Bernstein's own brand of liberal humanism is often reflected in his monthly economic letters. In the spring of 1968, for instance, he discussed the Administration's efforts to cool the overheated economy and reduce the unfavorable balance of payments by raising taxes and interest rates and reducing government spending. "The unemployed, in short, will make the major contribution to the preservation of our gold stock," he wrote. "Those who watch them riot this summer will do well to keep this aspect of sound finance in mind."

Harvard was the breeding ground for many of Bernstein's social and economic ideas. "It was the height of the New Deal when we were there," remembers Robert Heilbroner, who took economics courses with Bernstein. "We were passionately excited about it, and to study economics at this time was very inspiring." The relationship between the men was very close: they spent countless hours discussing economics, often on the way to double dates at nearby girls' schools. "We developed fantasies, assumed different personalities, we'd pretend we were interviewing famous economists on the radio," Heilbroner recalls. "We even had a secret language. Um keekee coon means 'I love you.' That's all I can remember." (Bernstein and Heilbroner still lunch together regularly every two weeks and read each other's manuscripts. Bernstein handles Heilbroner's stock portfolio.)

Bernstein graduated from Harvard magna cum laude and

Phi Beta Kappa in 1940, then worked for two years as an assistant in the prestigious research department of the Federal Reserve Bank of New York. During the war, he served in Europe as an Air Force officer—but actually more as a "working economist," selecting German industrial targets for air strikes. During this period he met, courted and eventually married in Wiesbaden, Germany, a secretary in the OSS named Shirley Dowd.

After the war, he taught banking for a year at Williams College, but he soon realized that to continue teaching he would have to go to graduate school. After some reflection, he rejected this idea. "I was twenty-seven, I was married, and I wanted to get going," he says. Another goad was his earlier life on New York's upper West Side with his brother and sister (now, respectively, art gallery owner Charles Alan and Aline Saarinen, widow of the architect and a critic/ commentator for NBC-TV). "They were both older and nobody ever had any time for little Peter," he remembers. "I was a slow starter. But now I've got the bit in my mouth." With a smile, he adds, "They never do anything now without consulting me."

So in 1947 he joined the Amalgamated Bank of New York, owned by the Amalgamated Clothing Workers, and soon he had assumed responsibility for managing both the bank's bond portfolio and its foreign department. Two years later, he joined the National Bank of North America.

Throughout this period, he steadfastly resisted joining his father's investment counseling business because their views of business and the economy were radically different. His father was a music lover who once wrote a book on the Ring of the Nibelungen, and had been an importer of sponges and chamois skins, a business he had inherited from *his* father, and then, with typical Bernsteinian serendipity, a partner in a Wall Street brokerage house, which was liquidated in 1933. The elder Bernstein had become known around the Street for his continual stream of free advice. After his firm went under, many of his friends told him that as long as he had so much advice to give he might as well make some money at it. Thus, in 1934 he formed an investment advisory firm with Frederick R. Macaulay, a recognized money-market authority. From its inception, the organization specialized in private individual and family accounts.

When Bernstein's father died in 1951, his long-time secretary, Sylvia Davidson, told the younger man, "You've got to go in there and hold the place together." He joined the firm that year as executive V.P. and learned the ropes from his father's partner, Linhart Stearns. But Stearns was twenty years his senior and in some ways even more conservative than the elder Bernstein had been.

Another problem, he came to realize, was the lack of a strong research staff. Traditionally, many firms such as Bernstein-Macaulay had been able to get by with only a smattering of investment intelligence; they depended on studies provided by the brokerage houses that executed their portfolio transactions. "Actually in those days you could make some pretty good judgments without explicit research if you had a working knowledge of economics," Bernstein says. "Surely, you could know, for example, that with the postwar housing boom in full swing building materials companies were a good thing, or that by 1957 oil stocks had been overbought in terms of any potential for further growth."

He soon came to realize, however, that investment counselors no longer could subsist on seat-of-the-pants evaluations, and he is convinced that his alliance in 1967 with the young, research-oriented firm of Cogan, Berlind was a positive step. Under the terms of the merger, Bernstein continued as head of Bernstein-Macaulay which operates as an autonomous subsidiary. He is also senior V.P. of Cogan, Berlind, and active in their management as well. Though his firm has full access to Cogan, Berlind research, he remains free to dispense brokerage anywhere he wishes, thus opening up additional sources of information. Less than 30 per cent of B-M brokerage is funneled through the parent group.

The merger is also pulling Bernstein gradually from the quiet, relatively easygoing world of family money management into the heady, wind-swept world of performance. The organization's activities have moved further and further away from the family business toward an institutional clientele, and he has had to make such moves as broadening the scope of a once-small speculative in-house mutual fund, the Bernstein-Macaulay Special Fund, to all of his accounts; he is even promoting sales of its shares publicly. The net asset value per share has substantially more than doubled in the past five years.

The many basic adjustments that have been required in both operation and philosophy, though they would constitute perhaps a deep trauma for many other men, have been a great exhilaration for Bernstein. "Before we had experienced a certain feeling of isolation, of remoteness, no matter how hard we worked to stay in touch," he says. "Now we're where the action is, right on the firing line in the markets." For him, finance will continue to mean people, not just money, but he admits that the new developments expose his firm more—increase its vulnerability—and that some of the old personal hand-holding relationships may no longer be possible.

"The difference now," he says, "is that life has another edge."

ED MERKLE
The McLuhan approach
to investing:
the premium is the message

OST MUTUAL FUNDS have offices in reasonably close proximity to the famed intersection of Broad and Wall streets, where the action is. But there is one fund located far away from Wall Street, in the vicinity of a different kind of action. The name of the fund is the Madison Fund, and its offices are on Madison Avenue. The location is very deliberate and very appropriate.

Unlike most funds, the Madison Fund is "closed-end." Open-ended funds stand always ready to sell new shares or redeem new shares. Sales and redemptions are made (not counting commissions) at what is called the "net asset value," or the total assets held by the fund divided by the total number of shares it has outstanding at any particular time.

A closed-end fund, on the other hand, does not sell or redeem shares once it has made its initial offering of stock;

and its shares are traded, often on the major stock exchanges, like those of any corporation. At any time one can figure the net asset value of a closed-end fund's shares, too. However, these shares always trade at either a premium or a discount of the net asset value, depending on how investors view the ability of the fund's managers to increase their fund's assets.

The majority of closed-end funds generally trade at a slight discount. The Madison Fund at the middle of 1969 traded, however, at a whopping 41 per cent premium, despite the fact that its performance has not been that spectacular. Why this outpouring of investor enthusiasm?

Let us listen to the philosphy of Edward A. Merkle, fifty-nine, a dapper, trim, distinguished-looking man with graying hair, who is the Madison Fund's president and chief executive officer. One of the main functions of a closed-end fund's president, he says, "is to get the fund so it's not selling at a discount. Otherwise you might as well open-end it." And how does one accomplish this? Merkle has one word: "RAZZMATAZZ." It is like seducing a girl, he goes on. "You have to be a salesman."

And a salesman he certainly is. He constantly strives for publicity—with a respectable degree of success. "We're in the papers continuously," he says. "The Madison Fund probably gets more publicity than all the other funds put together." Much of this derives from a seemingly unending torrent of speeches, which he will make almost anywhere at any time. "I love to make speeches," he says, and just to be sure everyone knows about it, Merkle employs a retinue of publicity men to alert the local press and stress that he will be available for interviews.

Much of Merkle's talent for getting attention is knowing what to say, and he cultivates the art of the quotable

aphorism, the spicy, controversial remark that always makes
good reading on an otherwise dull and colorless financial
page. He often makes specific predictions about the market,
and not long ago he was widely credited with being almost
alone in correctly calling a major turn in stock prices. "I
wasn't really that sure," he admits, "but I knew that it was
the time to say something and I knew that what I said would
be printed. It is more important to say something newsy than
be right all the time."

Another tactic Merkle uses to boost his premium is to hand
out plenty of capital gains dividends (distribution of capital
gains profit realized by the fund) to his shareholders. "Our
stockholders like dividends, lots of them," he declares, "and
that's what we try to give them." The advantage of receiving
these dividends is illusory, because the amount of the dividend is automatically subtracted from the fund's market
price. Merkle freely admits that the policy is a bit of financial
legerdemain. "It doesn't make sense, I grant you," he says.
"It's like taking money out of one pocket and putting it into
the other. But the stockholders are happy." Which of course
is what it's all about. Recently, Merkle has been handing
out about 10 per cent of his net asset value as dividends
against an average of 4 per cent for the other closed-end
funds. The impression that the Madison Fund is somehow
giving something for nothing is apparently widespread.
There is generally a significant rise in the premium right
before the periodic announcement of the dividend.

Merkle has been building up his promotional and financial
talents for thirty-two years. He came to the Street in 1925
and started his career in a time-honored way—as a runner
on the trading floor. While attending night school at New
York University, he progressed through a series of jobs as

230] THE MONEY MANAGERS

a security analyst. In 1949, while working for Mitchell, Hutchins & Co., Merkle joined Pennroad Corp., an old railroad holding company, which was an offshoot of the Pennsylvania Railroad Co. At the time the bulk of its assets consisted of special situations, often where Pennroad had representation on the board. Its operating record was lackluster, and so was the performance of its shares. Merkle took Pennroad over in 1957 and switched it to a new, faster track. He liquidated the bulk of its holdings and put the proceeds into a diversified portfolio of common stocks. In 1958, befitting its new look, Pennroad became the Madison Fund.

When Merkle settled into the president's chair at the Madison Fund in 1957, the shares were selling at a stiff 32 per cent discount from their asset value. It took a few years of work, but in 1961 the price finally swung over to the premium side and it has been upwards ever since. Since the current premium is about 40 per cent, and since the average closed-end fund sells at a 5 per cent discount, Madison's shareholders apparently are content to shell out 45 per cent more to have Merkle manage their funds.

"This is an age of images," is the way one analyst put it, "and for some reason, whether justified or not, Madison Fund has gotten itself a reputation as a go-go fund." Merkle disagrees. While he likes to do things with a flair, the flair doesn't go far as performance-fund philosophy. "We have to have some performance," Merkle maintains. "But our performance has not been spectacular and it won't be."

Between December 1958 and December 1968, Madison's adjusted net asset value per share has increased about 212 per cent, against a 61.6 per cent rise in the Dow Jones Industrials. In 1968, the results were 14.8 per cent for Madison and

4.3 per cent for the Dow. In both cases Madison was ahead of other closed-end funds but behind many open-end funds.

Merkle made headlines of a different sort at the Madison Fund's annual meeting in 1969, when he candidly admitted that during the first three months of 1969 "we had one of the worst performances I can remember in my twelve years as president." The fund was off 7.7 per cent compared to 5 per cent for the Standard & Poor's Index. Merkle admits that he broke one of the cardinal rules of the fund by not selling several stocks while they were at year-end height. "I wish I could have quit while I was still ahead early in '69," he says. However, he didn't want to take any more profits, he explains, for fear of leaving himself open for stockholder disappointment *next* year. Thus the value of his portfolio quickly dropped 15 million. A few of the fund's largest holdings were responsible for the dip—in particular, Denison Mines, Cities Service, Hartford Fire Insurance, Ward Foods, Pennzoil, and Katy Industries. Ironically, several of these same stocks were responsible for Merkle's good performance in '68. "We did very well playing the overall deal market, and that's how we got caught on Cities Service," he says. Merkle is holding on to these stocks, however, because he believes in their ultimate value. Typically, he is optimistic about the future. "When results for the year are counted, we will be · back in contention." In any event, investors have not minded 1969 results, because the premium has stayed at its lofty level.

What does he look for in a stock? "Growth and its relation to the multiple," says Merkle. "I generally buy into improving or takeover situations, for some special reason. For instance, the conglomerates, if you pick and choose, are good right now. I've been nibbling at some of them. A lot have been oversold. This accounting thing is silly. One of the big problems of the conglomerates is the horribly big supply of stock. In this case I think it's bullish to stop them from their acquiring for a while so they'll have time to manage and to spin off the ones they don't like." The fund, continues Merkle, has made a record of investing in second-line company stocks, what he calls "light blue chips." "In the kind of market we have experienced recently this group has been in some cases overdepressed because of the very thin markets. When the market turns, this type should show the greatest appreciation."

Merkle follows "ten simple approaches" to investment in deciding when to buy and sell. (1) He watches the stock recommendations and reports that flow across his desk each week. "If they run to three or four pages, everyone is bullish." (2) "The Federal Reserve Board writes the market letter. Whenever money is tight, sooner or later the market goes down." (3) His "stilt theory" says that when a stock has a straight line advance, he should sell—even at a risk of it's going up further. "I had an old aunt who said that the man who buys from me wants to make some money too." (4) For automobile stocks, he watches the figures on financing of cars—a lot of new financing, he says, signals that it's time to sell. Merkle also keeps his eye on: (5) the relationship of industrial prices to unit labor costs (6) the buying activity of open-end funds—when it's frenetic and high, the market is "a sale" (7) the cash positions of open-end funds (8) the discount or premiums on closed-end funds . . . a big premium is "a sell market" (9) the percentage of a stock owned by the funds—if it's as high as 35 or 40 per cent, avoid the stock and (10) finally, his own reaction: "How I feel in my stomach, how I feel when I wake up in the morning. When I think I really ought to forget it all and get out of the business, that's when the market rallies."

Recently Merkle has been unhappy that he has missed so many fast-moving glamor stocks, so he set a twenty-six-year-old to keep track of them and "scream and yell until we finally get around to listening to him." But even though he is watching the fast-movers, Merkle believes the "performance" philosophy is being overdone. "It was overdone in '62 and it will be again," he says.

If Merkle appears to be playing it pretty safe, he has a reason. For one thing, despite the market's performance in the late 1960's, he's convinced that it has yet to face up to one basic problem. As he sees it, a great deal of the market's fuel in the last few years (1966 being an obvious exception) was provided by relatively high corporate profits, made possible by three years of relative labor peace. Merkle maintains that unit labor costs are going up, at a time when the rise in prices is leveling off and the benefits of efficiency are diminishing. The inevitable result, he feels, is an old-fashioned squeeze on profits.

Though he is twenty-two floors above the corner of Madison Avenue and 60th Street, Merkle nevertheless has a good view of the goings-on at Broad and Wall. He sits on the boards of half a dozen companies (among them three portfolio holdings: Mid-American Pipeline, Missouri-Kansas-Texas Railroad, and Orange and Rockland Utilities, his fund's biggest single stock interest) and gets part of his feel for what's occurring on the business scene that way. Recently, he also joined the board of a French mutual fund ("They're highly bullish on our market"), which enables him to make periodic soundings across the Atlantic. A big part of his catch-up reading is spent in his chauffeur-driven car en route between his office in New York and his home across the Hudson River in Haworth, New Jersey, where he lives with his wife. Their two children are married; one is a twenty-six-year-old stockbroker.

For all his reputation as a flamboyant promoter and wily investor, Merkle appears a bit wistful as he sits at his desk among subdued Williamsburg furnishings. While he can't quite go along with the glamor stocks, he knows, too, that they're responding to the beat of a newer generation. As he muses out loud, "I'm fifty-nine and this is a young man's game. I don't know how it is going to be at sixty-five."

Ed Merkle may not exactly be the investment community's answer to Marshall McLuhan, but he is certainly giving the media-exposure route a game try. It seems to work in electing Governors and Senators in some states; it may just be the coming way to keep shareholders happy.

BILL O'NEIL
Truth from
the IBM 360-40

I T RATES YOUR STOCK PORTFOLIO, spouts investment maxims from Bernard Baruch and Gerald Loeb, and astounds even the most sophisticated of investors with its blinding speed. It seems to print good sound advice, like Ben Franklin did; like Will Rogers, it has a folksy, to-the-point way about it.

It's broker William O'Neil's stock market computer, an IBM 360-40-128K—a set of hardware, flashing lights, and investment chatter that covers perhaps a quarter-acre in the back of O'Neil's shop in Los Angeles. Like O'Neil—an ex-Texan, ex-mutual fund salesman, ex-customer's man for a large wirehouse who is now on his own with William O'Neil & Co., a New York Stock Exchange member firm—the computer is always optimistic.

"Every time there's a recession or a sell-off, the market

comes back even stronger," O'Neil says. "Sell-offs lay the foundation for new major moves."

Optimism and a computer may seem an unbeatable combination. At least so it appeared back in 1967. That's when O'Neil and his computer popped into the national investment consciousness with the baby-sized O'Neil Fund (assets: under $10 million), scoring a net asset gain of 115.7 per cent —thereby, according to a prestigious newspaper, "grabbing the brass ring" in the performance derby a percentage point or so ahead of the Enterprise Fund.

In 1968, the computer sputtered. O'Neil Fund scored a net asset gain of only 4.44 per cent, ranking 285th among all funds. By then, however, publicity on the performance had resulted in a flood of money. Assets had soared to over $45 million. O'Neil, the constant optimist, points out that the 1968 performance wasn't so bad, relative to the stock market's performance in general. In 1968, the Dow Jones Average of 30 Industrial Stocks rose 4.27 per cent; in 1967, the average had risen 15.20 per cent.

"If you make 115 per cent one year and you hold it the next year, that's not bad," O'Neil says. "Especially it's not bad in the market environment we had in 1968. I'll be very pleased to make 100 per cent one year and break even the next."

So despite a rough 1968 and some tough sledding in 1969, too, O'Neil still regards his way as the wave of the future. He still has the faith he had a couple of years ago when he bought the works—the IBM, the programmers, the necessary advertising outlays—in a kind of Texas wildcat parley. He says test clients who have stayed with him since 1960 have had a minimum gain of 500 per cent. O'Neil, who is thirty-six, puts it this way:

"We have the best computer system anywhere. We're years ahead, because we get it up with stock market people, not mathematicians."

O'Neil's computer system uses both technical and fundamental analysis. The system rates any portfolio it is given, and can present a manager with a whole variety of variables based on the five-year model it carries; variables such as price changes, volume and institutional sponsorship. For managed accounts, the computer gives the account's performance every month, rated against invested capital and Standard & Poor's. The computer even presents a completely posted account of gains and losses for tax purposes at the end of a year, so that the sheet need only be handed to a client's accountant.

"Pin down brokers," he'll say, his eyes downcast. "Ask them how much they've been making on the market themselves. Ask them to show you. Most of them lose, so do their clients." Most of the books in his personal stock market library contain only traditional lore, but O'Neil has them dog-eared and underlined. Now they have been absorbed and digested and, in part, programmed into the computer.

O'Neil seldom touches an over-the-counter stock and usually swears off anything below $20 a share, regardless of listing; yet he'll concentrate portfolios in one or two or three rapid high fliers. The reasons for avoiding low-priced stocks, he says, are that they rarely develop institutional support, and since they have volatile percentage moves, it costs too much to find out if you're wrong.

O'Neil himself plunged, to start, taking his entire personal winnings on the stock market in 1962 and 1963 to purchase a seat on the New York Stock Exchange in 1964. Perhaps this wildcat spirit can be traced to a Texas upbringing and schooling (Southern Methodist University); perhaps, too, to his abiding faith in (but not utter dependence on) the computer. "I don't believe in chance," he'll say. "Trace it, and there's a reason." Then he will relate a story of a neighbor in his sedate, upper-income West Los Angeles area who left both his Cadillacs in front of his house at night; he was robbed twice in a month.

O'Neil came to Los Angeles in 1958 with the mustering-out pay from a three-year Army stint in Alaska. Why? "I wanted to become a broker." Why Los Angeles? "Growth. For a broker, there is no better place in the world." He went to work at Hayden, Stone & Co. When his first child was born, he didn't have the money in the bank to pay doctor and hospital, but three years later he had a fund of $200,000. (There are now four children—three girls and a boy, aged one to nine.)

How? "Research," O'Neil says. I spent most of my time studying both fundamental and technical stock market approaches."

He also arranged discretionary agreements with his clients. When the massive break occurred in May, 1962, O'Neil was ready. He was 100 per cent liquid by March, and short by April 1. Then after the May break, he began buying Chrysler. That liquidated, with gains, he went heavily into Syntex, using all the leverage he could.

O'Neil wasn't buying for customers alone. He was also buying for himself. The parlay gave him better than a ten-fold increase. It was time, he decided, to get away from working for someone else. The entire winnings were invested in the seat and William O'Neil & Co. came into being early in 1964.

Most of O'Neil's reading time in 1963, when he was counting his gains and plotting purchase of a seat, consisted not of Baruch or Loeb, but of the Securities & Exchange Commission's massive, multivolume report on the securities industry. His copies of the report, like most of his books, now are bent, worn, and compulsively underlined. He wanted to establish a different type of firm, one that went beyond the traditional broker-client relationship.

"It has been our observation," he says boldly in sales literature, "that the majority of investors in the stock market have not made major progress. Many have lost money." Too many, O'Neil believes. And if brokers can't make it themselves—and many are money-losers—then how can they put clients into winners?

O'Neil decided upon some fairly unusual rules when he went on his own. He doesn't want the beginning investor. He doesn't want the account under $100,000. He scorns underwriters, secondary offerings, new issues and investment banking. He keys it all to the computer—although he doesn't really totally trust the beast.

"The computer is just a fancy adding machine, no better than the people you have. We don't buy a stock just because it shows up high on the computer print-out."

Under the O'Neil system, all listed stocks are programmed into the computer. Among the variable factors used are daily price changes, volume, quarterly earnings data, information on capital structure, and sponsorship by institutional investors. Every stock is rated on every variable and then assigned a composite rating, day by day. The bottom 90 per cent of the stock list is discarded.

Fundamental and technical analysis begins after the computer rating. Like a diligent self-help addict, O'Neil keeps vast scrapbooks with chart patterns of what he calls "successful stocks," ones that have turned around at certain points and at least doubled within a few months.

This means that like many technical analysts, O'Neil is a great believer in stock market precedent. If not, charts of the "successful stocks" would be meaningless. "Sure," he says. "Who doesn't believe in precedent? A lawyer goes to school to study precedent. So does a doctor. The stock market and individual stocks always are constantly repeating themselves."

He also keeps a "goof book." It contains chart patterns of stocks the firm has bought that have been poor performers. "Post mortem," says O'Neil. "It helps us to avoid repeating mistakes."

Although O'Neil now is armed with a computer, his investment philosophy really hasn't changed much from the early days. "What we look for," he says, "is change." By change, he means major shifts in earnings per share, new management, generally improved conditions in an industry.

Whether a company is new or an "old doyen" that's reviving, early spotting of the major change is essential. That's where the IBM comes in handy. "You must buy them when it's not clear to everyone that the change is coming. When you hear your friends talk about it, that means everybody's in it. It is time to get out."

O'Neil does not think salesmanship is his major talent, for he would like to be known as an analyst, but he doesn't hesitate to use the computer as a sales tool. This has some advantages: a cold, calculating machine that stores an incredible amount of information and blazes it out in seconds is of course looked upon with awe by customers; and the service can even be highly personalized.

A potential customer, submitting his portfolio, will get

a "thirty-second" run, which amounts to some 750 words. The portfolio is likely to be criticized. (If not, why switch to O'Neil?) Also, the potential customer's name will be used several times, and the computer will manage a few plugs for itself as a market analyst. For example:

DEAR MR. SEDERBERG:

OUR APPROACH IN ANALYZING YOUR PORTFOLIO HAS BEEN TO MEASURE EACH SECURITY YOU OWN AGAINST YARD-STICKS FOR STOCK SELECTION WHICH WE ARE USING DAILY IN THE MANAGEMENT OF OUR CLIENTS' PORTFOLIOS.

WE HAVE FOUND THE COMPUTER TO BE IDEALLY SUITED TO THIS KIND OF ANALYSIS. THE INVESTMENT OF YOUR CAPITAL IS ESSENTIALLY A PROCESS OF SELECTION FROM ALTERNATIVES AND COMPUTERS ARE JUST ABOUT PERFECT FOR RANKING ALTERNATIVES IN ORDER OF PREFERENCE—IF YOU CAN TELL THEM WHAT CHARACTERISTICS TO LOOK FOR.

MOST PEOPLE WOULD AGREE THAT EARNINGS GROWTH, BUYING SUPPORT OF MUTUAL FUNDS, NUMBER OF OUTSTAND-ING SHARES, AND A FEW OTHER FEATURES HELP DETERMINE WHAT A GIVEN STOCK WILL DO IN THE FUTURE. WHAT WE HAVE DONE IS TO PROGRAM INTO THE COMPUTER OUR JUDG-MENT ABOUT WHAT STANDARDS OF ACCEPTABILITY TO LOOK FOR AND HOW MUCH WEIGHT TO ASSIGN TO EACH OF THESE ELEMENTS IN RANKING INVESTMENT ALTERNATIVES.

After the portfolio is rated and discussed comes some philosophy. On stage, suddenly, are Bernard Baruch and Gerald Loeb, sandwiched between some basic lectures.

TO PARAPHRASE BERNARD BARUCH, HIGH PRICED STOCKS OFTEN ARE HIGH PRICED FOR A GOOD REASON—THEY ARE USUALLY WORTH MORE.

IF A STOCK HAS NOT BEEN ABLE TO ATTRACT PROFESSIONAL
INTEREST, THERE IS LESS CHANCE OF IT DOING WELL.

TO QUOTE GERALD LOEB: "CUTTING LOSSES IS THE ONE
AND ONLY RULE OF THE MARKET THAT CAN BE TAUGHT WITH
THE ASSURANCE THAT IT IS ALWAYS THE CORRECT THING
TO DO."

UNFORTUNATELY, MANY PEOPLE BUY GOOD CONSERVATIVE
STOCKS AND HOLD THEM FOR EXTENDED PERIODS OF TIME
DESPITE EVIDENCE THAT THEIR INVESTMENT VALUE IS
DECLINING.

The philosophy may be traditional, but getting it from
a machine that knows your name makes even calloused
prospects pay attention.

Computers in investment are still quite controversial.
They were even more so when O'Neil began to tinker with
them seven years ago. When his "computer management"
ads first appeared, (and he advertises widely and imagi-
natively), competing brokers countered with ads decrying
the merits of computers. Said one, "We don't feed our
clients into a computer and spew them out."

"I don't either," says O'Neil. As a matter of fact, he
really doesn't know computers, although he did pick up
some basics in a one-semester management development
course at Harvard Business School. "They tell me the one
we lease is an IBM 360-40 with a 128K memory, whatever
that is."

But he has a good idea what computers will do. That
includes, in addition to stock analysis and the customers'
monthly statements, the work on clearance and stock transfer. O'Neil isn't even sure how much he has invested in
computer operations. "Between $1 million and $2 million.

I guess we really haven't wanted to look closely at its cost to us."

Individual customers pay the firm a fairly standard management fee of 1 per cent on the first $100,000 in their account, ½ per cent on the next $900,000 and ⅜ per cent on the next $1 million.

O'Neil salesmen are not the typical producer-types in brokerage firms; they handle primarily institutional business. The firm has portfolio management contracts for twenty-five pension funds, and is investment advisor to several mutual funds. It manages, collectively, about $150 million, about half of it in institutional accounts.

Despite computer backing, O'Neil's methods frighten some of his customers. Usually the scare period ends after eighteen months, however, he claims. It takes that long to understand and the understanding often takes courage. O'Neil isn't afraid of selling at a loss.

"People who never sell are often taking greater risks and are really speculating in the market," he says, sounding like the computer's lecture. "The day comes when they're holding stocks at a loss. Usually by the time stock is down 10 per cent or 20 per cent, we want out of it. We don't believe in arguing with the reality of the market place."

He's made mistakes, he admits, and despite the temptation, he won't blame the computer. On one account, he made eighteen consecutive sales at a loss. "That client stuck with us," he says. "I simply couldn't believe it." The sticking with O'Neil or the eighteen consecutive losses? "Both."

Also the firm got back into the market too soon after the 1966 break. "We were kicked around for two or three weeks," O'Neil says, scowling slightly at the 360-40. "We weren't quite smart enough to pinpoint the bottom that time."

Three years later, in the early months of 1969, O'Neil's computer again failed him. He was selling in January and February, which, he says, proved to be the wrong thing to do. As a result, at an early point in the year, O'Neil wasn't too concerned. At midyear, he was saying, "Look, we could be down 50 per cent by July and still up 50 per cent for the year."

O'Neil likes the paper and building industries and hopes the computer will be instrumental in helping him spot what he believes will be two or three emerging industries over the next few years. "We know this," he says, "whatever emerges won't be the 1967–68 favorites. They won't be the Control Datas or the University Computings. There are young companies, new industries, new products cropping up all over the place. Consider that most mobile home manufacturers are under 10 years old and it wasn't even recognized as a separate industry until just recently."

A trio of O'Neil's winners in 1968: Graphic Sciences, Circuit Foil, National Homes. In late 1968 and early 1969, he was moving into the like of Varco, Inc. ("they have a gunsight that allows the military man to see in the dark"); Anodyne, Inc. ("young Florida company that has an anodizing process they've been able to sell to auto makers"); Gateway Sporting Goods ("we saw more teen-agers coming along, more leisure time for everyone"). One point: Most of them are young companies, in possibly new emerging industries. Speculative? Yes. O'Neil would be the first to admit it. But if one is the new Xerox, it would be worth it. "And there are plenty of new Xeroxes and Polaroids around today," O'Neil says.

The way O'Neil brings computerization to portfolio management differs in some major ways from the methods of
others. He uses it basically as a monitor and superstatistician,
and will often second-guess it. He does not use it for
"vertical" research into industries, with industry models.
The computer program's bias is basically technical.

Interestingly enough, the O'Neil Fund made its gain in
1967 primarily on computer stocks. Two of its biggest winners were Control Data Corp. and University Computing
Co. In fact, at one point, the fund had more than 10 per
cent of its assets in Control Data.

The computer, O'Neil says, has disproved several investment myths, and also has developed some new theories. For
one, it has shown that the growth stock theory may have
some loopholes. Most stocks poised for substantial advances,
O'Neil believes, are not those traditionally labeled growth
stocks. The computer has developed for O'Neil what he
likes to call the "old dog theory." By immediately comparing
various factors, the computer often shows when the traditional laggard dogs are poised for turnaround. Also,
O'Neil's computer—plus fundamental analysis and experience—has indicated to him that price-earnings ratios do
not really mean too much. More important is the quarterly
percentage increases in earnings.

One "research and development" question O'Neil is trying
to resolve via computer right now is the size problem.
Should a fund concentrate on forty or fifty stocks, as most
of them now do? O'Neil thinks it should not. "We're beginning to get evidence that in a $400 million portfolio, better
results are obtainable with a hundred fifty or so stocks
instead of fifty to seventy-five."

O'Neil does most of his thinking in an office adjoining his

home in West Los Angeles. The paneled retreat is furnished with sofas and soft chairs, desks, books and a proliferation of stock market equipment—a flashing electronic tape, quote machine, and a hot line telephone to his office. Here, where through a glassed-in wall he can view a tempting blue swimming pool, he hides away during the hours when the exchanges in New York are open.

No customers drop in for friendly chats, no telephones ring uselessly. The only interruption might be from a child, bringing a present ranging from a colored stone to a dead butterfly. Also, there is a small library of well-worn books. One of them is the life of Edison. "His scientific process was not unlike that which I think is coming to the stock market," O'Neil says, thumbing the book.

In his hideaway a mile from the Pacific and three thousand miles from Wall Street, O'Neil continues to believe that his way is the way of the future. He has five years' computer records of all listed stocks (he hopes to sell microfilms of them soon) and he believes that puts him way ahead. "Computer research," he says, "will be the dominant factor in the stock market within two or three years."

Back in his office, the 360-40 emits a barely audible hum.

GEORGE CHESTNUTT
The hidden secrets
of the big charts

HE THEORIES OF ROBERT RHEA? The Great Coyote
Hide Crash? Just how old are you, Mr. Chestnutt?

"Fifty-two and five-eighths, goin' on three-quarters," says
he, rippling a hand through a gray crew-cut "sprackled" on
his scalp.

That's old George with the put-on again, handling a
couple of visitors up from Wall Street for the day. Going
to Greenwich, Conn., is the only way to see George A.
Chestnutt, Jr. He's the master chartist, the manager who
has little use for the Street, whose American Investors
Fund runs on sheer chart-power. Whatever it is the charts
are whispering, Chestnutt listens well, because his fund has
been up there with the lean, long-striding performance
runners.

"Only get down to New York ten, twelve times a year, hate the place, always have, big dirty place. This is the closest I ever want to get to it. When I came East from Montana in '46 I spotted Greenwich and said 'there's a pretty spot.'"

Hate it he may, but this one-time lineman for the Montana Power Company has eight direct lines plugged into brokerage houses in the big city. He has to. By 1970—'71 at the latest—Chestnutt confidently expects to be head man of a billion-dollar mutual fund empire.

Not bad for a maverick who only started in the fund business eight years ago with net assets of $30,000—that's not even the bid price on a low-income split-level in Greenwich, Larchmont or any place else.

In the first eleven and a half months of its life, his American Investors Fund caromed from $30,000 to $1,320,000. And it's doubled five times since.

Even in the bad year of '66, a late-starting sales drive pushed the fund's net assets from $58.3 million to $85 million. "Yep, we just keep on doubling," Chestnutt says, thumping one of his ever-present charts, "and by now I suspect we're already up to $120 million."

In 1966, after twenty years as an investment advisor operating out of suburban Larchmont, Chestnutt made the big corporate move to Greenwich. In planning the headquarters of what he hopes will be a billion-dollar investment company, Chestnutt, in typical fashion, had the building designed by the man who did his own home in the suburban Connecticut town.

As for Wall Street, he not only feels he can live without the air pollution—he can do without the atmosphere, too.

Doesn't he miss the stimulation of his colleagues and competitors? With a gesture toward his wastebasket, he answers: "Why I've thrown more original research into the circular file than they've done in their entire lives. I can say four out of five times whether a stock is going to go up or down the next day—and when I don't know I'll tell you."

Yes, but how about the information flow in the world's most respected investment community? "You can put a baboon at the helm of a space ship but you aren't going to get anything intelligible back . . . it's a garbage input and garbage output."

Chestnutt insists he's been doing his own financial thinking ever since the happy days as a teen-ager in a home hacked out of solid rock on the shores of the Missouri River in Montana. His father and namesake ran a substation for the power company "and by '26 he was playing the market— you know the usual things, utility shares, Great Northern, Anaconda."

There in the wilderness, George Jr. began learning about the stock market. Looking back on it now, he sounds something like Young Abe Lincoln with a Point-and-Figure chart. "The operator of the local bucket shop in Helena taught Dad how to keep charts. He did for a week and then said, 'Here George, you do it.'" He was twelve then, and the biggest thing he had to look forward to was going out every fall to bag a deer or an elk of his own. "Oh, yeah, I used to go after coyote hides too. I remember at the '29 top they were bringing $30. In '32 they were down to 50 cents."

In Helena High, Chestnutt apparently acquired his life-long drive to be the valedictorian. He ran a "mutual fund of sorts with $75 of my own, $100 apiece from two other kids and something like $250 from my father. We did all right I guess; anyhow, I remember we broke even when the fund busted up at graduation time."

Along with the local market in coyote pelts, everything was riding high at the '29 top, including his father who was worth about $30,000 on paper in the market. Then he borrowed $3,800 against it to take advantage of a rights offer. Two years later, his portfolio was worth only $3,800 and the bank was getting worried. " 'You know me,' my father told the banker, 'I'm George Chestnutt, I never beat a bill in my life.' So they let him pay it off at $100 a month. He was only making $200."

About this time George Jr. was getting ready to go out and lick the world. But first he had to pitch hay for ten cents a day. College was put off for a while and he took a fifth year of high school, studying everything he hadn't hit before "until they finally kicked me out of cooking and sewing."

In those days the young Westerner had the idea he'd become a research chemist and try to make vaccines out of petroleum. "But I soon switched to electrical engineering when I realized that a chemist would probably have to work for du Pont and go East."

Somewhere along the line, probably in the local paper which he consulted for its abbreviated stock list ("sort of a Gallup poll of the market"), Chestnutt came across an ad for the respected Robert Rhea technical service. He bought one trial subscription after another and started boning up on the Dow Theory. "I read all I could. Compared with chemistry, I figured, technical analysis was in a position that chemistry had been in fifty years earlier."

The foundation was laid. At the age of 52% Chestnutt runs

one of those geo-, electro-, atics, -ism, -onics funds that is willing to take a flyer on anything—so long as it moves. But he makes no bones about looking like some bull-market Babbitt. His club is the Rotary of Larchmont; on his wall he flaunts a Chamber of Commerce award; he voted for Goldwater "because we had no choice"; he starts the day with the Greenwich *Times* because the other one is "too pink."

Looking out at the world through his four-sided spectacles, Chestnutt has been developing that market approach full-time since 1946 when he came East to plunk down $5,000 for a one-third interest in the Mansfield Mills Company, an investment advisory service. Five years later he became the sole owner and changed the name to the more evocative American Investors Company. Ten years later this was changed to "Corporation" and last year all assets were transferred to Chestnutt Corp., investment advisors to his American Investors Fund and to private individuals willing to pay a minimum of $500 for quarterly market advice. (It's a $35 million business now but the fund last year overtook it on the profit side of the ledger.)

Chestnutt is the closest thing you can find to a pure chartist among the men running the nation's major mutual funds. Frankly, fundamentals scare him.

In his detailed, red-covered pamphlet, "Stock Market Analysis—Facts and Principles," the investment advisor is as chatty and outspoken as he is in person, a rare attribute among Wall Street types.

"Should I buy a stock that pays an unusually high dividend return?" asks one headline. "No!" shoots back the author, "This practice is very dangerous!" (The last time an exclamation point was spotted in an advisory book it turned out, under chemical analysis, to be a fly speck.) As Chestnutt explains his antidividend stance: "The usual reason behind a high dividend yield is that informed investors are distrustful of the company's ability to maintain the dividend rate over a period of years."

"Fortunately we do not need to know *why* one stock is stronger than another in order to act profitably upon knowledge of the fact," the book goes on. "The market itself is continuously weighing and recording the effects of all the bullish information and bearish information about every stock. No one in possession of inside information can profit from it unless he buys or sells the stock. The moment he does, his buy and sell orders have their effect upon the price. That effect is revealed in the market action of the stock." In other words, hidden inside the past performance of a stock, like genes inside the human cell, is information about the future. Thus while others see a stock as a collection of employees, factories, products, advertising campaigns and so forth, Chestnutt looks only at the numbers, which have a life of their own.

Chestnutt devotes a great part of his solitary mornings of forecasting to the supply-demand lines, that is, the places where his brown, blue, red and green chart lines tell him the buying should come in. By plotting an individual stock's action on ratio-scale paper, he gets a "geometric" look at what it's really been doing. In other words he's more concerned with its percentage gains and, coincidentally, how much volume it took to move the issue up or down a point.

Back in 1948, the lean and lanky Westerner was sprawled out on the couch thinking about a favorite—for him at least—subject: relative-strength ratios for all stocks.

He sprang upright to his usual position—something akin

to a bar chart—and concluded that the only way out of the dilemma was to come up with his very own 800-stock geometric average of the stock market.

Until then, he claims, every known average, including the Dow which he was nurtured on, was often so far off that four-fifths of all stocks were either stronger or weaker than the index that supposedly reflected their average performance.

Under Chestnutt's guiding principle, every stock is weighted equally. Then each industry group is weighted according to the number of stocks in it (rather than some fundamental approach based on an industry's history, size, profits, assets or trading volume). Thus, by August 1, 1966, the Chestnutt 800-stock average was led by electronics with a weight of 5.63 per cent, then oils at 5.13 and all the way down to the bottom 0.38 ratings of beryllium, bowling, soft drinks and fertilizers.

The average's founding father insists that some analysts prefer his group indices especially because they include marginal companies that are "more sensitive to changes in competitive condition, giving advance warning of impending weakness near the tops of group movements."

A lot of penny watching goes on in the neat Colonial brick building at 88 Field Point Road, Greenwich. Behind a facade which could pass for that of a D.A.R. Post, Chestnutt's expanded staff of fifty keeps up with the mass paper-shuffling of a fast-moving investment company. "But I'm the analyst," says the boss, "backed up by the IBM which doesn't have employee status but should."

Chestnutt runs charts on over a thousand stocks and will expand to two or three thousand as soon as his new trading room is ready. After the group trends, his second major tool is his computerized run-down of "position-timing ratings" for individual stocks. Every week the computer following Chestnutt's preordained formulas ranks 800 stocks in order of their relative strength. The top 8 get a 99 rating, the next 8 are 98, and so on down to zero. On the basis of these, and various market-timing approaches, the advisory service tells its subscribers what the best buys—and even short sales—are for the week. But much of the Chestnutt approach is locked up behind that open Western smile. For instance the degree of the overall market's bearishness or bullishness is traced on a mysterious curve called "the trend oscillograph." All that is known is that its creator feeds it "market statistics known to contain clues to probable future market action" and from them he creates moving averages covering different time periods. What kind of clues?

Well, Chestnutt says they range from price changes of leading stocks, upside and downside volume, odd-lot figures, daily sales, brokers' loans—anything. "I'd like to be more precise"—Yes! Yes!—"But I can't." Oh. "It might save the competition five years."

Parboil away the fat and here is what the Chestnutt recipe seems to be calling for:

"You've got to get in the boat with the guys who've been right . . . to find the ten stocks most likely to double in the next year you've got to start with a look at those that've doubled in the last year and especially look at those that've doubled three years in a row . . . 'Recovery stocks?' If I looked I probably couldn't find any. And if they recovered they'd probably go back to where they were in a few weeks."

Like most "performance fund" managers, Chestnutt finds

he has to hop on the same stocks that are making new highs every day or are otherwise attracting a speculative following.

As the manager of an institution doesn't this worry him? "If you have hold of a kite and you let go, that's the most dangerous thing."

And how has his high flying been going? "I can give you 62–38 odds on what any stock is going to do in a day," he goes on. "But it's hard to make money because of the brokerage-house commission bite. I bawl out my traders if they don't get a stock at the low for the day or sell it at the high. What we really try and do is keep the specialists out of it. The job of my traders is to find the actual seller and four out of five times they can do it. I don't mind getting on a queue when we're buying an active stock. When you're first on line it's fine; if you're last you can get a horrible whipsaw."

To live by the word of such old Chestnutt chestnuts, his traders find themselves leading a rather hectic life. Outside, kids are lazily taking set shots in the Greenwich High School yard across the street; a troop of birdwatchers goes by; a gardener gently plants crocuses on the lawn of the neighboring Tudor-style house. Inside, three stock traders from the suburbs are trying to pull off a $1.7 million trade without tipping off every hot-stock watcher on the Street. The portfolio turnover is an indication: around 50 per cent.

On the second story of his almost-Colonial mansion, Chestnutt sits in seclusion, the only diversions are a Pan Am calendar, a print of the white water in some Western river, and a gently ticking Federal-style clock. Occasionally he'll punch a stock symbol on the desk-top quote unit or get up to trace a thick finger over his master wall chart, which has been extended twice and seems in danger of crawling out the window if this market keeps up its hectic pace.

Mr. Chestnutt, sir, to what do you attribute the apparent success of your portfolio management? "We hold the happy people stocks."

Excuse me? "They're the stocks the public sold at a profit. And you know this is all a game of mass psychology— it really hasn't changed from my father's day forty years ago and it's no different whether it involves Chinese, French-men or Germans. People will always readily buy back any stock that they made money in before. Happy people. Happy people stocks."

To make his point, Chestnutt trots out a chart which he handles with the reverence of a museum custodian touching papyrus. But he refuses to decipher the hieroglyphics of half a dozen different colored lines which would seem to be leading indicators on their way toward pointing out bottoms and "psychological" buy-points.

From 9:30 A.M. to 8 P.M., Chestnutt works at plotting his charts. Every Thursday night he works till 3 A.M. or so— "memorizing my charts," he says—to get ready for the chore of churning out the weekly market advisory letter. "I think I'll double the fee," he says.

"In the fund business my big job is to beat Fidelity," the Boston-based fund run by the famous "Mister Johnson," he points out, "and they've been subscribing to my stuff for seventeen years."

Chestnutt says he's not much worried about the com-petition from anybody. "The typical fund manager com-mutes in from Darien or Jersey with other fund managers, reading his *Wall Street Journal*. He's an expert, he has lunch with the other experts, and how does his broker get his ideas: The same way. It's no surprise to me that the typical fund manager has trouble beating the Dow. Whenever he decides to do something, he has to have six out of nine men on a committee to approve it."

Chestnutt stretches and ends another day with a drive home to the place that looks quite a bit like his investment trust's headquarters. His wife Sara cooks dinner. He has no servants. His daughter and adopted son live thousands of miles away. He asks Sara what's new.

Afterword

I F YOU HAVE BEEN DILIGENT, you will by now have read about nineteen men who, to a greater or lesser degree, are practitioners of the great new investment philosophy of performance. You will have discovered how this philosophy is revolutionizing the investment policies of institutions holding many hundreds of billions of dollars. It is perhaps appropriate at this point to speculate briefly on whether performance is merely an ephemeral quirk or whether it is destined to persist even after the last few reluctant dollars hidden in mattresses and cookie jars have been rooted out and flung into the latest hot movers.

If the past is any key, the need, or the desire, to perform will tend to propagate itself. Few money managers today can afford to ignore the growing demands of clients and shareholders for superior results (even if they wanted to—

most of them don't). Unfortunately, these demands may begin to enmesh the performers in an inevitable statistical trap. It was comparatively simple for Jerry Tsai and other pioneers of the performance era to do well because opportunities among good growth stocks with rosy futures were plentiful. Today, though, there are burgeoning legions of ambitious money managers anxiously scrutinizing lists of available stocks with slide rules, computers, charts and vast networks of analysts and other informed sources. Inevitably, fewer issues are priced alluringly out of line with their future prospects, and it is becoming harder to do consistently well in relation to everyone else. A leader of the pack one month in one kind of market, perhaps as a result of some lucky fluke, may soon find himself lagging far behind. Everyone's performance, meanwhile, increasingly begins to approach that of the market averages, a tedious prospect indeed. In the sharp bear market of the first half of 1969, for instance, most of the heroes of 1967 and 1968 ignominiously did just as badly, if not worse, than the Dow Jones Average. Such vagaries may subdue the enthusiasm of mutual fund shareholders and possessors of institutional capital and cast doubt on the entire philosophy of performance, at least as it is now understood. Maybe the widely-acclaimed new breed of portfolio managers will become so exasperated and frustrated that they will withdraw en masse and take up something less harrowing, such as politics.

At the moment, however, most of the men portrayed in this book, and most especially the "stars," are too busy with their portfolios for much indulgence in these contemplations. They are of course acutely aware that their world and their special knack for spotting winners are subject to rapid, fundamental metamorphoses which they may be totally unable to anticipate and, to be sure, they sometimes muse about what the future may be like. But they also know that the best way for a star to protect himself against the wrinkles, cracked vocal chords and other infirmities and calamities of tomorrow is to act and sing his heart out today.

The Institutional Investor, in which the articles in this book originally appeared, is a professional magazine with a controlled circulation of 21,000 money managers who are responsible for the security portfolios of such institutions as mutual funds, pension funds, banks, insurance companies, universities and foundations. Collectively, its readers guide investments of some six hundred billion, and they account for about 50% of all the trading on the New York Stock Exchange. Though unavailable to the general public, the magazine's lively, often irreverent approach has won acclaim beyond the boundaries of Wall Street during its two and a half years of existence. "It is breathless with the drama of high finance," wrote *Newsweek. Time* said the magazine is "fast proving that writing about finance can be both exciting and amusing," and that "money managers find it hard to put down." According to *Playboy,* it is "the jazziest, most candid, most interesting of all the literature about mutual funds."